D0805412

HANDBALL

About the author

Michael Yessis was born in New York City and grew up playing one-wall hand-ball until he came to California and was introduced to four-wall handball. It has been his love ever since.

He received his B.A. and M.A. degrees from the City College of New York (now CUNY), lettering in lacrosse and soccer. After serving in the United States Army and doing biological research, he attended the University of Southern California where he earned his Ph.D. degree.

Besides playing handball for many years, Dr. Yessis is considered an expert in analyzing skill technique. In part, this is due to his specialization in bio-mechanics and due to his study of technique analysis of various sports, as done by scientists and coaches in the U.S.S.R. For the past fifteen years he has translated Russian articles dealing with technique analysis of select sports and the training of high-level athletes. Many of these articles are published in select journals in the United States and in the *Yessis Review of Soviet Physical Education and Sports*, which has world-wide circulation.

Dr. Yessis is listed in such sources as *Who's Who in the United States*, *Who's Who in the West*, *Dictionary of International Biography*, *Men of Achievement*, and *Leaders in Education*.

HANDBALL

Physical Education Activities Series

Michael Yessis
California State University,
Fullerton

THIRD EDITION

Wm C Brown Company Publishers
Dubuque, Iowa

Consulting Editor

Aileen Lockhart
Texas Woman's University

Evaluation Materials Editor

Jane A. Mott
Smith College

Copyright © 1966, 1972, 1977 by Wm. C. Brown Company Publishers

Library of Congress Catalog Card Number: 76-46016

ISBN 0-697-07076-X

Printed in the United States of America

Contents

Preface

This book is designed for all persons who wish to improve the caliber of their handball. Processes involved in the theory and practice of handball from beginning through top-level stages of development are presented. The book not only explains how the game is played, but also provides reasons for various kinds of play. In addition, cinematographic analyses of many shots are presented to give detailed explanation of what occurs when the ball is hit.

The material is presented in clear-cut stages beginning with the fundamentals of handball and progressing to the highest level of skilled participation.

Interspersed throughout the book are self-evaluation questions designed to challenge your thinking and to help you evaluate your progress as you move toward top-level play. You should not only attempt to answer these questions, but also pose additional ones as a self-check on learning. Since the order in which the content of the text is read and the teaching progression of your instructor are matters of individual decision, the position of evaluative materials may not always correspond with the presentation of given topics. In some instances you may find that you cannot respond fully and accurately to a question until all the material has been read more extensively or until you have gained more playing experience. From time to time you should return to such troublesome questions until you are sure of the answers or have developed the skills called for, as the case may be. Handball is a game of strategy—you must *think*.

The history of handball

1

Handball is considered to be the oldest of all the games played with a ball. The present-day game is of Celtic origin and began in approximately the tenth or eleventh century. The game first appeared in Ireland and is believed to have been brought there from France where it was probably learned from the Romans since the Romans are known to have played a form of handball in the *thermae* or baths of Rome. During the time that France was occupied by the Romans a game of handball known as bare-handed pelota appeared. This game is still played in many parts of southern France. Some historians also believe that tennis originated from a form of handball in which the ball was hit back and forth over a net.

During the sixteenth and seventeenth centuries, the game came to be called Fives. It became very popular in the Emerald Isle in the midnineteenth century when many town and country championships were held. Of interest is the fact that the courts were from 50 to 60 feet long, 25 feet wide, and 30 feet high. The front wall was made of slate and the other walls of cement or smooth concrete. The ball was made of strips of rubber and yarn wrapped around a very small cork center covered with a fine layer of horsehide and sewn as a baseball. The ball was smaller than a baseball, but much faster than the standard handball in use today. Players were allowed to kick the ball and developed much finesse in this skill as most low balls were returned by kicking. This practice continues today in Ireland where the players are allowed to kick the ball on the second bounce if it is not returned by hand on the first bounce.

In the recorded history of this game the greatest champion was probably John Cavanagh who played during the early nineteenth century. It is written that he was superb in all aspects of the game, and upon his death not one player remained who was his equal or even second to him in skill. Cavanagh's successor in the midnineteenth century was William Baggs who introduced scientific methods of hitting the ball so that it would curve and hop. Baggs is often considered the father of modern handball as his methods of hitting the ball provided the foundation for a new era of handball.

Many great handball players migrated to the United States from Ireland in the late nineteenth century. Phillip Casey is perhaps the best remembered in this country. His enthusiasm and talent did much to stimulate a large following for the sport. In 1887 he played John Lawlor, the Irish champion, for the world championship and a purse of one thousand dollars. The match was to be decided by the winner of eleven out of twenty-one games, the first ten to be played in Ireland and the last eleven in the United States. The score after the first ten games was six to four in favor of Lawlor, but after returning to the United States and playing before large crowds, Casey won seven straight games and thus gained the championship. He retired in 1900, still undefeated after successfully defending his title many times. Michael Eagan, who succeeded Casey, won the first Amateur Athletic Union Handball tournament and therefore became the first official champion of the United States.

In the early twentieth century handball developed into two distinct games: the one-wall game, which can be considered a truly American version, and the four-wall game, which was modified in terms of court dimensions and type of ball used. In both games the original hard ball was replaced by a softer ball—a tennis ball with its outside covering removed. Most players wanted a faster ball, a desire that led to the development of a small gas ball. This ball was in turn modified and became the ball we play with today—a smaller, heavier, much faster ball. Both games require most of the same basic skills and strategies, although modifications must be made for the different playing areas. It can truly be stated that after players have participated in either version they usually fall in love with the game. Present-day handball players are quick to say that they have yet to know of anyone who, after playing the game, does not like it.

The one-wall game originated along the beaches of New York City where bathers found hitting a tennis ball against the open walls of the bath houses with their hands an excellent game. Because one-wall courts were relatively inexpensive to build compared to four-wall courts, the number of one-wall courts increased as did the number of adherents to this game. Bleachers capable of seating two to three thousand spectators were erected, increasing the popularity of the sport. One-wall handball is so common today in New York City that almost everyone who grows to maturity there is exposed to the game. This is not to say that the game is uncommon in other areas of the country, for the game, with innovations and modifications, has spread to all states. In California, for example, a three-wall version is played in some schools and playgrounds. The front wall is the same as for the one-wall game, but two cutdown side walls are added so that the more varied front-wall play can be seen. A recent innovation in New York City combines the one- and four-wall elements of play in a three-wall jai-alai type of court. There is a front wall, a back wall, one side wall, and an open side for spectators. Other courts consist of only a front wall and two full side walls.

The four-wall game, which is played in most cities, was slower to grow but gradually spread west from the eastern seaboard. Credit for this spread is given to the Detroit Athletic Club, where several indoor courts with wooden floors were built. In 1915 this club held the first invitational four-wall tournament, which was won by Fritz Seivered of Cleveland. Bill Ranft of the Los Angeles Athletic Club, using the new softer ball, won the first Amateur Athletic Union National Championship only four years later. This shows how rapidly the popularity of the game spread across the country.

New York City is considered the stronghold of the one-wall game for both men and women. It is interesting to note that in the one-wall game the service is one of the most important shots and players work for many aces. Because many handball players in the East play the one-wall game, they naturally spend a great deal of time developing a strong serve, even when they also play the four-wall game. This fact may explain why eastern players emphasize the serve and western players emphasize court maneuvers and kills.

Even a brief summary of the development of handball in the United States would not be complete without mentioning the contributions of Robert Kendler and a group of handball enthusiasts. In 1951 they helped form the United States Handball Association (USHA), which is considered a players' fraternity, originated for and by players. This organization has been responsible for promoting the game throughout the country.

Today the number of participants continues to increase. For many years only men played the game, but now women also enjoy the sport. To accommodate the greater number of players colleges and universities, as well as athletic clubs, YMCAs, recreation centers, and other similar organizations, continue to construct new courts. Many of the new courts have glass walls to accommodate many more spectators (most older handball courts have only a small balcony high in the rear wall for viewing). However, the advent of racketball (a game identical to handball except for use of a racket and a slightly larger, softer ball) has caused a serious problem concerning the use of handball courts. Because racquetball is played on a handball court, there is once again a shortage of courts for both handball and racquetball players in many parts of the country.

Because handball has both English and American heritage, many of the terms are common to the game on both continents. You should learn and use these terms properly so that you can talk the game of handball. You should use correct terms so that you and your opponent will clearly understand each other during play and during any subsequent discussion of rules or play.

When you talk about handball to a foreigner, be sure to explain that it is not the same game of handball popular in Europe. European handball, or team handball as it is commonly called in the United States, is played on a field or in a gymnasium.

What is handball like?

2

Handball is one of the simplest, yet most challenging, games known to man. The rules are easy to learn, and you can quickly understand the game once you see it in progress. Handball may be played by two (singles), three (cutthroat), or four (doubles) players. It may be played on a one-, three-, or four-walled court. Various types of games are possible. Most of the material presented in this book applies to all variations, but major concern is given to the four-wall game, which is both the most complex and the most thrilling (a debatable claim) of the games.

   The four-wall game is played in an enclosed room in which all four walls are playable. The room consists of front wall, two side walls, rear wall, ceiling, and floor. Visualizing yourself enclosed in this relatively small room (fig. 2.1), pitted against an opponent and a fast-moving ball bouncing in unexpected

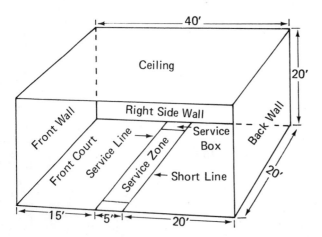

Fig. 2.1 Court Dimensions and Nomenclature

Which form of handball do you think provides the fastest play: one wall? three wall? four wall? What advantages can you see in the different forms? What disadvantages?

directions off the floor, ceiling, side, and/or rear wall can give you an idea of what is involved in the fast game of handball!

To start the game one player, the server, stands within the service area, bounces the ball on the floor, and as it rebounds strikes it with his hand with sufficient force so that it will rebound off the front wall and strike the floor behind the service zone before it strikes either side wall, the ceiling, or the rear wall. The opponent must then return the ball in such a manner that it will hit the front wall before it strikes the floor. Either hand may be used in hitting the ball; the ball may be struck only once on its return. If the ball is not returned by the opponent, and if the ball has been legally served, the server scores one point. During play if the server fails to return the ball, he loses the serve. His opponent then becomes the server, and he becomes the receiver. The first side to score twenty-one points wins the game.

The ball may be played after one bounce or it can be volleyed as it comes off a wall. During play, the ball may strike the side walls, the rear wall, and/or the ceiling on the rebound from the front wall or on a return to the front wall. A ball that has bounced twice on the floor may not be played. When this occurs, either a point is scored for the server or a hand-out is called, depending upon who served the ball at the start of play and who failed to return the ball prior to its second bounce.

In doubles, each partner is given an opportunity to serve before a side-out occurs, except in the case of the initial service when only one partner serves. The purpose of this rule is to help prevent a strong doubles team from winning a game before the opponents have had an opportunity to serve. In doubles, the ball must be returned alternately by the receiving side and the serving side. Either player on a side may return the ball.

To play an effective game of handball it is necessary to have the proper equipment. Because handball requires little equipment, each item becomes very important and at one time or another may be the crucial factor in winning a game.

The basic equipment includes regular gymnasium wear, tennis shoes (sneakers), handball gloves, and official ball. When choosing your gymnasium wear, it is essential to remember that your shorts and shirts must allow for total movement and must not feel tight. Clothing which restricts arm or leg movement will in turn prevent you from executing a full swing or not allow for the necessary bending, twisting, and running. For maximum leg movement the shorts should be slit up the side, while the shirt should be sufficiently loose around the shoulders to allow for a full range of motion. Your shoes should fit well and not be loose. If your feet slip in your shoes, not only may you lose a fraction of a second in getting started on a fast side cutting movement, but you also put excess stress on the ankle joint. Blistering of the feet can usually be prevented by wearing two pairs of socks. If you play on concrete or wooden floors for any length of time and your legs become excessively sore or begin to ache, you should wear Ripple-soled shoes. Because of their greater shock-absorbing ability, these shoes protect wearers from the pounding effect of these surfaces and help keep muscles relaxed. The increased traction created by the ridged soles of these shoes also gives you greater maneuverability.

Handball gloves, which must be worn at all times during play, help to keep the hands free of perspiration and protect them from injury. The gloves are made of leather, horsehide, pigskin, or goatskin. They have a strap, adhesive material, or elastic band to keep them snug around the wrist. It is very important to choose gloves that fit very snugly around the fingers and hand. If they are loose, you will have trouble keeping them on after play starts, for the gloves will stretch when they become damp from perspiration. If your hands perspire excessively, you should wear cotton inserts to prevent the gloves from becoming wet and loose. It is important to rinse the gloves in water occasionally to wash out the salt from perspiration which accumulates in the gloves. If this is not done, the leather gets hard and stiff and soon cracks. When first beginning handball, a player will find it worthwhile to use gloves with padded palms to help prevent bone bruises. As your hands become accustomed to hitting the ball, however, you should wear gloves with but a single thickness of leather in order to get better feel and control of the ball. To help prevent bone bruises or hand soreness you should soak your hands in hot water for a few minutes before beginning play. This practice increases circulation in the hands and causes tissues to expand. The expanded tissues act as a cushion when your hand contacts the ball and protect the underlying bones and blood vessels.

If you wear eyeglasses, be sure that the lenses are unbreakable and that the glasses are firmly secured with an elastic retainer so that they cannot come off during play. It is recommended that players who do not wear eyeglasses use wire or plastic eye guards made especially for handball to help prevent injuring the eyes. Getting hit in an eye with a ball traveling fifty or more miles per hour can be very dangerous. You should protect yourself with guards, of some sort, irrespective of your playing ability.

Aside from the basic athletic wear, the only extra equipment necessary is a ball and a pair of leather gloves as required by rule. In four-wall handball, a black rubber ball 1⅞ inches in diameter and weighing 2.3 ounces must be used.

Of the various sports human beings engage in handball probably ranks among the top ten in terms of the number of values that can be derived. More all-around body development and physical fitness are involved in this sport than in most other sports. All parts of the body are used and are essential: both arms and hands, shoulders, waist, legs, and feet. A greater amount of energy expenditure is required than in any other individual or dual sport. Consequently one can achieve or maintain a high level of physical fitness by merely playing handball several times a week. Because handball requires quick mental responses to constantly changing game situations, the game is also valuable in developing fast decision and reaction abilities.

The most outstanding attributes which can be developed by regular participation in handball are muscular strength and endurance, cardiorespiratory endurance, agility, flexibility, decreased movement time, symmetrical development of the body, and improved timing and neuromuscular coordination. Handball is especially effective in maintaining a trim waist because it requires so many flexing and twisting movements. This strenuous and exciting sport requires and leads to the all-around fitness advocated so strongly by top medical and physical education personnel. Total fitness is essential for successful living. This condition allows an individual, regardless of occupation, to perform daily tasks with much greater ease and effectiveness.

Participation in handball helps to develop the lungs, heart, and blood vessels and probably even more important increases the ability of the body to recreate and/or strengthen its restorative processes and metabolic functions. These factors are responsible for growth of new cells and tissues, the prolongation of youth, and continued function of all body systems at a high level. Participation in handball exercises all body systems which in turn adapt to the great demands placed upon them and are thus strengthened. Of very great importance is that a player feels mentally and physically relaxed and satisfied after a game of handball.

Handball is now popular with many businessmen who have little spare time and are under tremendous mental strain. Through this sport, these men find relaxation and maintain top physical ability, both necessary for effective job performance. Handball is also played by people in diverse occupations; astronauts for example, participate in handball to maintain physical condition. Handball is played by athletes and coaches during off-season in order to maintain fitness, to improve quickness of movement, and/or to develop strategy similar to that required in their respective sports.

The sport is played by people of all ages, for intensity and frequency of participation can be varied according to objectives, interests, and needs. Nor is handball limited to men; many women play four-wall handball and a larger number participate in single-wall handball.

Although handball has gained tremendously in popularity during the last decade, growth in this country has been relatively slow. Perhaps one reason is that very few people have been able to watch a game in progress because spectator facilities are generally lacking. This situation is now being remedied. An increasing number of handball courts, which provide open or glass-enclosed galleries for spectators placed high in the rear or the side walls are being constructed.

There never has been a controversy about one thing: experienced players wholeheartedly agree that once you have participated in handball you will continue to come back for more, be it for fun and enjoyment and/or for the biophysical values to be derived!

Essential skills

3

It is important that you have correct body, arm, and hand position in order to be able to hit the ball well. These prerequisites aid in achieving effective ball contact, sufficient force, and control necessary for accurate placement. If you concentrate only upon hitting the ball, without regard for the necessary form, the result will be frustration. Your shots will be weak and wild and will usually result in easy returns for your opponent.

For executing most shots your hand should be held in a relaxed position with your fingers bent slightly in a cupped position. Your fingers should not be held together tightly because this will cause a tight wrist which makes impossible the complete flexibility needed for most hits. The ball should be contacted with the base of the fingers and the upper palm of the hand. The ball is slung or thrown from this contact position rather than just hit by your hand. As a beginner you may experience some difficulty with this action, but do not be discouraged; ability can be developed in a relatively short period of time if you practice correctly. Most beginners find while learning that many of their hits are made in the palm of the hand or off the fingers. This is normal as most hits will inadvertently be contacted in these areas while eye-hand coordination is developing. After some practice, however, you will find it easier to contact the ball on the base of the fingers and you will develop the feel of throwing or slinging it. Good and poor ball contact positions are shown in figure 3.1.

In preparation for returning the ball stand relaxed facing the front wall with your arms at ease. As your opponent prepares to begin the serving or hitting action, you should assume the ready position, a position from which it is easy to move in any direction while preparing for the return hit. To assume the ready position bend forward slightly from the waist and unlock the knees. Do not bend the knees excessively or go into a deep crouch as this will cause you to lose time when going into action. Raise both arms slightly so that your forearms are almost parallel to the floor and the elbows flexed to form a forty-five to

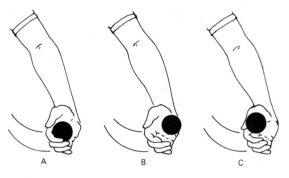

Fig. 3.1   Ball Contact Positions: **A**, Good Position; **B** and **C**, Poor Positions

ninety degree angle. Feet should be shoulder distance or more apart. There are many slightly different ready positions, but the basic concepts of each are the same. Many times the ready position which you assume will be determined by the play going on or by your physical condition at that moment. Examples of the ready position are shown in figures 3.2, 3.8A, 3.17A, and 5.4A.

In the ready position your weight should be borne in the middle of the feet and not on the balls of the feet. Having your weight (center of gravity) over the balls of the feet and holding this position for a second or two creates tremendous tension in the muscles of the foot and leg. This in turn will put you off balance and you will not be relaxed. When your weight is borne on the middle of your feet, you are in the most advantageous position for moving in any direction. However, after your opponent hits the ball and you see that you have to move forward or forward and to the side, immediately shift your weight on to the balls of the feet so that you can move as quickly as possible in the desired direction. If you see that you have to go to the back corners or to the back wall, straighten the body which thus enables you to move more quickly to the rear.

When getting ready to hit the ball, you should always be in a position to swing your arm freely without feeling cramped or tight. When you are in a relaxed position with your arms free to swing, you will have time to think where you want to hit the ball, and even more important, you will have effective con-

Fig. 3.2   Examples of the Ready Position

trol of your hits. Facing a side wall is the best position for most shots. When hitting a right-handed shot, you should therefore be facing the right side wall with your left hip pointed toward the front wall. The opposite is true for a left-handed shot. Your hitting position is probably the key point for you to remember because it will determine the outcome of your shots in most instances. To get into the best hitting position you must have good footwork, an outstanding characteristic of all top level athletes in all sports.

HITTING THE BALL

The actual swing and hit is a highly coordinated neuromuscular act requiring precise timing of powerful muscular contractions in a proper sequence of actions to produce maximum velocity of the hand and fingers. The force and momentum generated by each joint are transferred to the next adjacent joint and culminate in your hand, thereby allowing you to achieve maximum force and speed. In other words, you are trying to get a summation of internal forces working from the large musculature of the leg, hips, trunk, and shoulders out to the smaller muscles of the arm and hand.

All the actions involved in hitting the ball can be broken down into four phases: the preparatory or backswing phase, the power or forward swing phase, the contact phase, in which the ball is in contact with the hand, and the concluding or follow-through phase. Although each phase is distinct, overlapping portions of each are present in the total swing action. Also, modifications of the basic motions in each phase take place when the ball is hit underhand, sidearm, or overhand, but the same basic principles apply.

Preparatory Phase

In the preparatory phase backswing movements take place in order to prepare for the forward swing actions. It is necessary to get into the correct hitting position and to use proper backswing movements in order to execute good hits. This means that from the ready position you should turn to a side-facing position while maintaining a slight crouch, shift your weight to the rear, rotate the hips and shoulders to the rear, bring the arm back to a position in line with or behind your shoulders, bend the elbow of the rear arm, and hyperextend (cock) the wrist while keeping the fingers slightly curled but relaxed (fig. 3.3). All these actions are done sequentially, beginning with the foot and working up to the hand.

For example, if you execute a right-handed shot, hitting the ball waist high or below in which you move in on the ball, you perform the following sequence of movements. Start the action by turning the right foot so that the toes point toward the right side wall, with the body weight on the left leg (fig. 3.4, A). As this action is being completed, abduct the left hip joint and then push off the left foot by extending the knee and ankle joints in order to shift the weight to what is now the rear right leg. To abduct the hip joint move the hips

Fig. 3.3   The Backswing

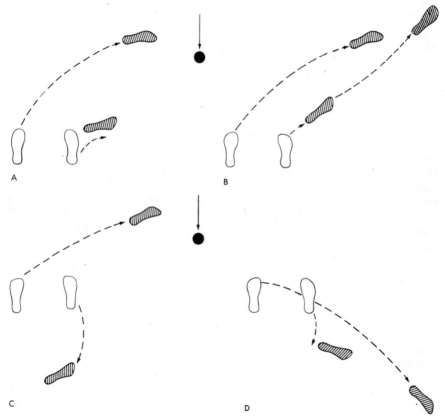

Fig. 3.4   Footwork Patterns: **A**—One Step, Moving in on the Ball; **B**—Two or More Steps, Moving in on the Ball; **C**—Deep Hit, One Step in on the Ball; **D**—Deep Hit, Two or More Steps to Get to the Ball

and shoulders as a unit over the rear leg. As you do this, rotate the shoulders to the rear, bend arm, and then cock the wrist. As these actions take place you must keep looking at the ball.

It is good practice when you try for correct body position to anticipate where the ball will be when you make contact. Read the path of the ball and then position yourself accordingly. For example, if you see that there will not be ample time to move in on the ball as just described, you then follow the pattern outlined in figure 3.4, C. In this situation, for a right-handed shot you step back with the right leg and simultaneously point the toes so that they face the side wall when the foot is planted firmly on the floor. Then shift your weight onto the leg in the manner described in figure 3.4, A.

To position yourself properly, especially during singles play, it is necessary to take several steps to be where the ball will be before you go into all the hitting actions. For example, on a right-handed shot if you have to move forward or forward and to the side to reach the ball, you turn and step out with the right foot toward the spot where you will make contact with the ball. This maneuver should consist of one short step followed by one or more running steps until you reach the ball. If you have to go to the rear on a right-handed shot, you simultaneously step to the right with the right leg and turn to the rear and immediately take one or more running steps (fig. 3.4, B and D).

Power Phase

The power phase begins prior to completion of the preparatory movements. As the arm and hand are brought to the rear, forward weight shift begins. Start the weight shift by stepping in the direction of the oncoming ball. For a right-handed shot you step out with the left leg (fig. 3.4, A and B). For the most efficient hit you should step out at an angle of forty-five degrees, that is, toward the front and side walls from a side-facing position. The toes of the left foot should also point in this direction. On a fast ball coming directly toward you step directly toward the front wall. If the ball goes deep, step to the rear, and if the ball is to the side, you step directly toward the side wall.

In order to step out you must extend the ankle and knee joints and abduct the right hip to shift the weight forward. This action, known as stepping into the ball or getting your body into the hit, is very important for the production of power. As you shift your weight forward, it is vital that the rear foot maintain contact with the floor until the ankle and knee are fully extended. If it does not, the momentum generated by the body will be lost. To absorb the weight of the forward action of the body, the left leg, after making contact with the floor heel first, flexes at the ankle, knee, and hip joints. The amount of flexion is determined by the amount of weight transference and by how low the ball is. The length of the stride is likewise determined by the height of the ball. If the ball is contacted low, a long stride is taken; if the ball is contacted waist or chest high, a moderate step forward is taken.

As forward weight shift is completed, forward rotation of the hips occurs and is followed by forward rotation of the shoulders. It is important that shoulder rotation be maximal in the hitting position assumed prior to beginning movement of the arm. Only in this way can the muscles be put on stretch, which is necessary if the muscle group is to have a powerful contraction. Once the shoulders have rotated so that the upper body is facing the front wall, the arm begins its forward action, with the elbow leading and the forearm and hand still to the rear. As the elbow comes in line with the body, elbow extension begins, but the wrist remains cocked. As the hand lines up with the elbow and the body, wrist action occurs (fig. 3.5). There are several distinct types of

Fig. 3.5   The Swing

wrist action whose use is usually dictated by the stroke being used, by the position of the ball in relation to the body, and by the effect you wish to impart to the ball. Although wrist action begins prior to ball contact, the main actions occur during contact. These actions are explained in the discussion that follows. Visual descriptions are provided in figures 3.6 through 3.22 (sequence of action through the moment of contact should be studied carefully).

Contact Phase

Initial contact with the ball occurs when the ball is in line with the hips or in line with the center of the body after the body has been transferred forward—in other words, in line with the body when the body is in its final position ready for contact and not where it was when you first started the backswing movements. The ball remains in contact with the hand for about 1/80 second, and when it leaves the hand, it is in line with the forward leg. During this contact time, the ball is compressed and immediately expanded, which puts it into flight and adds to the force gained from the moving hand. With such a short period of contact any wrist action that occurs must be very fast. This is why before attempting to impart any "stuff" to the ball you should have the necessary muscular development.

During contact if you want to hit the ball without putting spin on it, you should flex only the wrist using very little carry time or maintain a firm wrist. To do this, keep the palm of the hand perpendicular to the floor during con-

What kind of spin and rebound result when you come across under the ball? when you come across the right side of the ball? How can you avoid putting spin on the ball?

tact. If you want to impart sidespin to the ball so that it rebounds sharply to the right or to the left as it comes off the front wall, you should come across the ball from behind to the right or to the left. The ball should spin clockwise on a vertical axis (when viewed from above) in order to rebound sharply to the left and spin counterclockwise if it is to rebound sharply to the right. If you come across **over** the ball during contact, you will impart topspin which will cause the ball to rebound higher off the front wall, and if you come across **under** the ball during contact, you will impart backspin to the ball which will make it rebound lower off the front wall. However, every time you put spin on the ball, it will travel slower. To be most effective in your strokes you should not constantly use only one kind of wrist action. The path of your hand during ball contact should remain level or in a straight line if the hit is being directed upward or downward. As you try these different wrist actions, you will discover that both the left and right arms must be used in order to produce all the different kinds of spin.

When hitting the ball, hit it hard; do not hit easy except to execute specific shots or when the play calls for it. Many players when first learning a skill that requires speed and accuracy mistakenly believe that they should hit easy until they can control the ball and then hit harder. However, it has been proved that speed and accuracy are developed most effectively through practice of both skills at the same time, and this is what you should do.

Follow-through

As soon as the ball leaves your hand, the concluding movements or follow-through phase, begin. This part of the swing is as important as any other phase even though the ball has already left the hitting hand. If you stop the swing at the moment the ball leaves your hand, continuity of your swing will inevitably be disrupted. When you stop the swing too soon, the muscular braking action causes a decrease in the force and momentum generated. In addition, the hand will not be in the desired position if the swing is stopped too soon, and this will cause the ball to travel in an unpredictable direction.

In the follow-through all body movements follow the hand. As the hand follows the ball for a short period of time, the arm comes forward first, followed by the shoulders, hips, rear leg, and foot until you finish in a position facing the front wall prepared to assume the ready position. After the handball has left your hand, your swing should be continued until it stops of its own accord. This will occur naturally. Do not strive to finish in a particular position advocated as being the most worthwhile. All players finish their stroke differently, although the strokes usually look similar. The follow-through is demonstrated in the final sequences of figures 3.6 through 3.22.

The most important phases of the swing are the power and contact phases. It is not critical that you look a particular way in the preparatory and follow-through phases except as how position relates to what you do during the power and contact phases. For most effective hits, however, it is imperative to execute all phases of the swing to the fullest extent. This includes the backswing when the body is wound up and the arm brought back, the forward swing where power is generated as you get your body into the hit and unwind with strong shoulder rotation, the contact phase when speed and spin is imparted to the ball, and the follow-through to ensure force and smooth continuation of movement.

In practice—and much of it is required—it is not necessary for you always to hit a ball to develop this swing. You may go through the motion by thinking of the separate phases and then imagining the execution of the total move. Learning involves the development of correct pathways from your brain to your muscles. As practice of these motions continues, the pathways become stronger. You will become more relaxed and experience less fatigue, for you will have eliminated unnecessary tension and unnecessary movement. When your swing becomes smooth and well coordinated, it will no longer be necessary for you to think of what you have to do. When you have learned the swing, it becomes an automatic act.

After hitting the ball, you return immediately to the correct court position in anticipation of the return made by your opponent. If you do not wear eye guards, you are put in the dangerous position of being hit in the eye by the ball. This fact must be remembered in order to avoid serious injury to the eyes. Your main responsibility is to get into position for the return—which requires that you follow the ball—therefore, it is essential that you wear eye guards.

THE BASIC STROKES

The foregoing analysis and description for hitting the ball apply to all the basic strokes. Except for minor modifications in your body and arm positions, you use the same fundamental swing for executing all of the strokes described in the discussion that follows.

The Underhand Stroke

The underhand stroke is used in many shots which are hit very low at approximately knee level or below. Many top players do not use the underhand stroke because it is more difficult to direct the ball on a level or downward plane. Also it is not possible to get maximum power because the amount of hip rotation and elbow extension is limited. However, there are a few outstanding underhand hitters who have great shoulder strength and so use this stroke effectively. Underhand strokes are most often used for low placement on the front wall

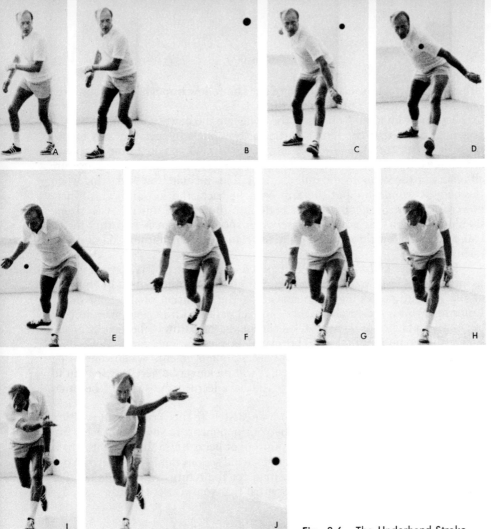

Fig. 3.6   The Underhand Stroke

when hitting from the front court and for high placement from the back court, although this shot is very difficult to control. The underhand stroke is also used quite often when fast play does not permit sufficient time to get into a side-facing position, usually when a player is up close to the front wall.

In the full underhand stroke your body is crouched with sufficient lean of the upper body and bend in the knees to ensure proper hand contact with the ball (fig. 3.6). Your arm is kept relatively straight (but not stiff) on the backswing until it achieves extension in the vertical plane. It remains thus on the downswing and follow-through, keeping close to your body when the hit is made. Your hand, which circumscribes an arc in the vertical plane, is kept in a slightly cupped position, with the wrist firm throughout the swing. Many times as contact is made the fingers may open up if you are trying to keep the ball low. The performer shown in figure 3.6, G demonstrates this reaction. However, it has no bearing on the outcome of the shot since the ball is contacted in the palm of the hand. If contact is made on the fingers, the resulting hit is much softer. As proficiency in this stroke increases, you should add wrist action in order to impart greater force to the hit or to put spin on the ball. Also, in execution of this shot it is imperative that you maintain good eye contact with the ball, as does the performer in figure 3.6. Notice how he still looks at the place of contact long after the ball has left his hand (sequence I).

The Sidearm Stroke

The sidearm stroke is the most important stroke in handball. It is used in the majority of shots which are hit approximately between chest level and knee level when a player is in a crouched position (fig. 3.7). In preparation for the hit bring the forearm back fairly level to the floor, with the elbow flexed (sequences A-C). As you step into the swing (sequences A-D), have the weight shifted onto the front foot (fig. 3.7, E). As you complete the shift, rotate the shoulders to the front (sequences D and E) and bring the arm forward, with the elbow leading (sequence E) and the hand cocked. (In this figure the performer does not have his hand cocked, probably because he is putting top spin on the ball.) As the hand approaches the middle of the body, some elbow joint extension takes place (sequence F). The amount of elbow joint extension depends upon how far the ball is from the body and whether spin is to be put on the ball.

For maximum power and little or no ball spin, extend the elbow fully during the contact phase. If the ball is fairly close to the body (approximately one to two feet away), the elbow should be extended proportionately. If you want to put spin on the ball, the elbow should remain flexed. During the contact phase only the hand is in motion and the body is held in a stable position (sequences F and G). After the hit take a full follow-through (sequence I), and after stepping down with the rear leg, you automatically are in the ready position for the next shot. (Other examples of the total swing are shown in figs. 3.9 through 3.17, 3.21, 3.22, 5.4, and 5.7.)

The Overhand Stroke

When the ball is above your head, use the overhand stroke. To execute this stroke raise your arm up and back in a vertical plane as you shift your weight to the rear by dropping the rear shoulder after assuming the side-facing position. To do this, merely flex the spine laterally (bend over sideways). This action is the same as for throwing a baseball or football. As the forward swing begins (after the weight has been shifted forward and the hips and shoulders have been rotated forward), the elbow should lead as it does in the other two strokes. If the ball is well above your head, your arm should straighten prior to hitting the ball (fig. 3.19). If the ball is at approximately eye level, your arm should remain flexed until after you have made contact. After the hit is made, the arm is extended and should be straight on the follow-through (see figs. 3.18 and 3.20).

Fig. 3.7 The Sidearm Stroke

At times it is advantageous to hit the ball so that it will travel in a horizontal plane toward the front wall with great speed. The ball may also be hit in a downward direction, but this shot is more difficult to control, and you should avoid it until you have mastered the high and level hits. When contacting a very high ball, direct the ball so that it will hit on the ceiling close to the front wall or high on the front wall. You should take a full follow-through and execute the entire swing in a vertical plane. To help ensure a high hit assume a position under the ball, which requires additional bending of the body toward the rear.

Combination Strokes

As the ball cannot always be hit in the ideal position with respect to distance from the body and height at the moment of contact, variations or combinations of the basic strokes are sometimes used. If the ball is a few feet away from your body and below your knees, for example, use an underhand-sidearm stroke. If the ball is high but away from your body, a sidearm-overhand stroke should be used. In general, the farther the ball is from your body the more the sidearm stroke should be used, in combination with the underhand when the ball is quite low and with the overhand when the ball is fairly high. An example of the sidearm-underhand stroke is shown in figure 3.8.

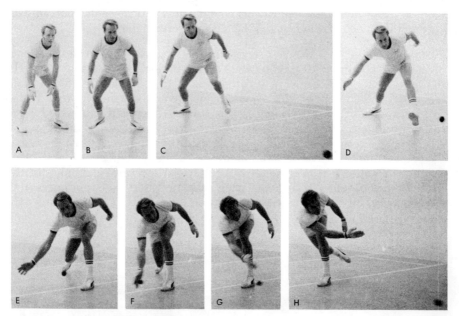

Fig. 3.8   The Sidearm-Underhand Stroke

It is essential that you learn the basic strokes before you can hope to achieve any degree of proficiency with the various combinations. In order to master the basic skills it is very important that you assume the correct position each time before hitting the ball. It is therefore necessary for you to learn to judge where the ball will be. Judgment and anticipation are very important aspects of handball and should receive your attention from the beginning.

USE OF THE BASIC STROKES

The Service

As in most other dual sports the serve is often the determining factor in losing or winning. It is therefore most important to have a strong, effective serve. All of the basic strokes are utilized in serving. Consequently the effectiveness of the serve depends upon the skill with which you can execute the basic strokes. As your skill increases, your serves will become stronger. During the serve you have the advantage of having ample time to think of which serve to use, where to hit the front wall, and what speed or force is necessary in order to achieve your purpose—that is, to score or at least to hit the ball in such a manner that your opponent will have difficulty in returning it. You should look at the serve not merely as a means of getting the ball into play, but also as an important shot requiring your deliberate and calculated thought. Various shots you can execute on the service are discussed in the following paragraphs.

The Power Serve   The power serve, which utilizes the sidearm stroke, is one of the most common effective serves. You hit the ball hard so that it travels to the rear corner. Your opponent is then forced to make his hit after the ball rebounds off the floor, for there should be no rebound off the rear wall. If the ball is hit higher than anticipated, it may still be effective if it is placed close to a side wall or if your opponent has to play it from a crowded position in the rear corner. In each case you will have inhibited your opponent's swing.

   To execute this serve well, you should be positioned fairly close to and facing the side wall in a deep crouch, well bent over at the waist, and only slightly bent at the knee joints so that your hand is below the level of your knees (fig. 3.9, B and fig. 3.10, B). This position helps ensure a low hit on the front wall

Fig. 3.9   The Power Serve

and increases the possibility of getting your full body momentum into the shot. The ball should be released from your hand at a low height so that it will not rebound high, and the hit should come when the ball is momentarily stationary, at the top of the bounce. The ball should be bounced away from the body so that the arm can swing freely and not be impeded. Remember that you step into the hit; therefore, the ball must be bounced to a position where it will line up with the hips after the weight has been shifted (fig. 3.9, D and fig. 3.10, E).

Weight shift should occur during the time that the ball is released as you step into the hit. Note how the player in figure 3.9 takes one step, while the player in figure 3.10 takes two steps, in moving into the hit. Two steps help to put the body in motion, thus generating more momentum and as a result greater power. However, both performers have very good weight shift as indicated by the unweighted rear leg and the greatly tensed forward leg.

The player in figure 3.9 gets most of his hitting power from shoulder rotation and arm action (sequences C-F), while the performer in figure 3.10 utilizes much hip and shoulder rotation along with arm action (sequences E-G). However, it is not necessary to have hip rotation when low balls are hit. You should maintain a good crouch, and when you do, it will be very difficult (if not impossible) to rotate the pelvic girdle. In order to execute hip rotation you must raise the trunk and/or keep the waist and hip joints extremely flexible, and have great lateral lean. The player in figure 3.10 does all of these actions as he rotates the pelvic girdle for more power.

In general, the greater the number of body parts involved in the act the greater is the power. However, accuracy and control are sacrificed. Since most serves require both power and accuracy, it is advisable to cut out rotation of the pelvic girdle to help ensure a bit of both. Also coming through with the hips, as the player in figure 3.10 does, places you in a less favorable follow-through position. The tendency to lean back after the hit redistributes the weight onto both legs. From such a position it takes longer to go into action for the return hit. The player in figure 3.9 is in a much better position to move after the next hit or to assume the ready position.

Both performers have good body action and make good contact. The player in figure 3.10 has better wrist action (note the cocked wrist in sequence F and the strong flexion throughout the contact phase into the follow-through phase in sequences G through I), while the player in figure 3.9 has a firmer wrist. If he were to use more wrist action, the hit would be much more powerful. However, he still hits the ball very hard because of his size. The performer in figure 3.10 is much shorter, and perhaps that is the reason why he uses hip rotation and greater wrist flexion to get more power in his hits.

To keep the ball low it is necessary to have a long low follow-through. This stroke is demonstrated in figure 3.9 E and F and in figure 3.10, H and I. To hit the ball to your opponent's left arm, you serve the ball from the right side of the service zone and aim at center or left of center on the front wall so that the ball will rebound toward the left rear corner. This serve is diagrammed in figure 3.11.

Fig. 3.10 Weight Shift During the Power Serve

The Lob Serve   The lob serve, effective as a change of pace, is almost the extreme opposite of the power serve. The ball is hit easy and makes a high ballistic flight to the rear corner. For a lob serve you should aim to hit high on the front wall, using an underhand swing that contacts the ball low on the initial bounce or using an overhand swing that contacts the ball high over the head from a high initial bounce. The underhand stroke is easier to control, however. Both techniques are effective, but the high hit ball of the overhand stroke carries higher for a longer time, and its path is not as curved as in the underhand stroke. The ball in either hit should have sufficient impetus to just reach the rear wall after rebounding off the floor. It will then drop sharply. The receiver usually swings impatiently at this seemingly easy floating setup or else gets caught in a position where he cannot use a complete arm stroke in his return because the ball is close to the side wall. You will find this serve especially effective when your opponent is keyed up and ready for a fast moving ball.

To execute a lob serve position yourself in the center or slightly on that side of center in which you want to hit the ball. You should hit the ball in such a manner that it will rebound directly toward the rear corner. The ball should hit the floor in midcourt and then bounce into the corner (fig. 3.11, B). Some players stand very close to the side wall when serving the lob, but this position takes greater control in hitting the ball so that it will not hit the rear side wall and bounce away where it becomes a potentially easy shot to return. You can see that with these two serves a variety of returns are possible, and for these the server should always be prepared. The ball can be returned on a fly, a half volley (immediately after striking the floor), a bounce off the floor, or a rebound from the rear or side wall. You should also be aware that for every serve on one side of the court there is also an identical serve on the other side of the court. Each should be attempted and mastered if possible, for a large, effective repertoire of serves is essential to a top performer.

The Diagonal Serve   As proficiency is gained in the power and lob serves, you should then begin to develop the diagonal or Z serve. In order to gain the maximum power and control necessary for proper execution of this serve, the player uses the sidearm stroke, although he can also use the underhand or overhand stroke. In order to hit the ball to the left rear corner you should position yourself close to the left side wall in the service zone, facing toward the right front corner. You then strike the ball so that it will hit the front wall approximately two to four feet from the right side wall, depending upon which hand is used in serving. When it rebounds from the front wall, the ball develops counterclockwise spin, and the spin is further increased as the ball comes immediately off the side wall in the front corner. The ball should then bounce in the back court. Because of the existing spin, the ball when it hits the left side wall rebounds almost parallel to the rear wall. If the rebound is very close to the rear wall, as it should be, this serve is then very difficult to return (fig. 3.12).

The diagonal serve is most effective when hit low and hard enough so that the necessary spin will be generated when the ball rebounds out of the front

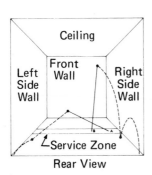

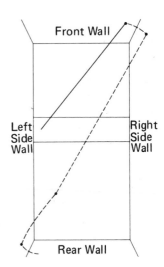

Fig. 3.11   **A**—The Power Serve; **B**—The Lob Serve

Fig. 3.12   Top View of Diagonal Z Serve

corner. It can also be executed from a high bounce (fig. 3.13), and when this is done, the player attempts to hit the ball high on the front wall in the same pattern as for the underhand stroke, but at a different height. In this case the ball is not hit hard, however, and because of its slower speed the ball drops sharply in the back court close to the rear wall and is therefore difficult to return.

Because of the sharp rebound angle of the low, hard-hit diagonal serve, it is very difficult to return when it bounces off the floor. Thus, most players are forced to play it off the side wall or possibly off the rear wall. It should be remembered that the server is out of position when executing this serve, so as server you should move immediately into the middle of the court after hitting the ball. You should hit the diagonal serve to either corner, depending upon your opponent's weaknesses.

The Angle Serve   Almost all serves are angle serves, for the server always attempts to place the ball where it will be very difficult if not impossible to return. One of the most effective spots toward which to serve is the rear corner, close to the wall. Several additional serves, difficult to return, can be used to achieve this placement. Most of these serves can be hit with underhand, overhand, or sidearm strokes, but the sidearm stroke is preferred. For these serves the server stands in the same position as for the preceding serves; this similarity provides a desirable bit of deception.

One of the most effective angle serves is to hit low and hard, hitting the ball to the front wall a few feet on the far side of the center of the front wall so that it will hit the side wall a few inches from the floor just beyond the short line (the back boundary line of the service zone which divides the court into

Fig. 3.13 The Diagonal Serve Using the Overhand Stroke

two equal halves). The ball will rebound off the side wall very low and fairly sharply so that it is difficult to return. If an opponent gets his hand on the ball, his return is usually soft and quite high. An ace, a ball that eludes the receiver, usually occurs if the low, hard-hit ball strikes the junction of the side wall and floor at the same time. This is called a *crotch shot*. If the ball hits floor and wall simultaneously from a very low angle, it will not rebound sufficiently high to allow its return, or it may rebound at an unpredictable angle (fig. 3.14).

You should be able to serve the ball at an angle so that it will hit the front wall approximately four to five feet high and then rebound off the side wall at approximately this height just beyond the short line. The ball then bounces deep in the back court and carries to the rear wall toward the far corner where it rebounds to the opposite side wall, but not very sharply. The ball has a tendency to hug this side wall especially if it has lost most of its original momentum and drops sharply because of the spin generated. You should remember that every time the ball hits a wall it loses some speed. In this serve the ball hits three walls after rebounding off the front wall and is therefore slowed down considerably. This serve, commonly known as the *scotch serve*, is difficult to return if properly placed. To play the ball after the bounce, the receiver must retreat deep into the back court, and this action usually puts him off balance. You should not hit this serve too high or too hard, for if you do, it will come out of the corner in a way that makes an easy return possible (fig. 3.15).

Other Serves   Another effective serve is the *straight corner* shot. Your initial position in the service zone should be about six feet from the side wall. You should hit the ball at about knee height, approximately three or four feet from the corner on the front wall on the same side so that it will rebound from the floor deep in the back court, hitting the rear wall six to twelve inches away from the corner. Upon rebounding off the rear wall, the ball should travel very close to the side wall. Your opponent will usually be hesitant about taking a full

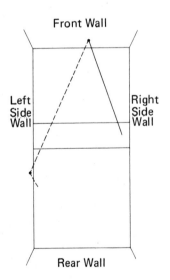

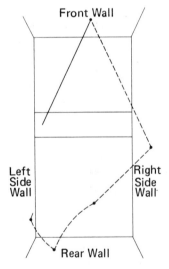

Fig. 3.14   Top View of the Low Angle Serve

Fig. 3.15   Top View of the Angle Serve (Scotch Serve)

swing on his return for fear of injury. If he does hit the ball, his angle of return will be very small, and as a result his return is weak. A ball that comes straight off the back wall rather than go into the corner is an easy shot to return.

The same reasoning can be applied to the lob serve. The ball in this case drops sharply as it remains close to the side wall after rebounding off the rear wall. Both the straight corner and lob shots, however, are vulnerable because the receiver has a chance to return the shot before the ball ever reaches the rear wall. He may choose to volley the lob shot, or he may return the low shot off the bounce before it hits the rear wall. Either response may give him an advantage: by getting off a quick return he may catch you off balance.

Service Strategy   You should strive for a high degree of effectiveness in one or two serves, but should not rely solely upon these. If you do, your opponent will be able to prepare himself because he will know what to expect. It is important for the same reason to change both the speed and the area to which the ball is aimed. Changing speed is very important, for this throws off your opponent's timing. If you vary only the type of serve, never its speed, your opponent will quickly adjust to this speed and have greater success in retrieving all balls regardless of variation in location on the floor or wall.

Try various serves, various speeds, and various placements. If you follow the general guidelines presented here, you will have some degree of success even from the very first attempts. Precise accuracy will not be achieved at the very beginning, for accuracy requires much practice. However, if you direct most of your serves into the rear corners where they will be difficult for your opponent to return, mix up your serves in both placement and speed, and have one or two well-developed serves to use in the clutch, you will be well on your way to becoming a top-level player.

The Playing Shots

After the ball is served, you must use basic shots to score a point. The most lethal of these is the kill shot, and next in order are the passing shot, the ceiling shot, and the lob. Although the kill is the most effective offensive shot, it should be remembered that any one of these shots may be equally effective in achieving the major purpose: to hit the ball away from your opponent so that he cannot return it or to draw him out of an advantageous court position. To execute these shots successfully, you must satisfy one prerequisite: the proper positioning of your body so that your entire swing can be performed as previously described. The most frequent error made by beginners is neglecting to position themselves for the next shot, and therefore their shots are weak and/or wild. The forthcoming shot looks so easy that these players relax and as a result must attempt the shot either from a flat-footed position or by rushing at the last minute. You should position yourself so that you can return the ball efficiently and effectively.

The Kill Shot   There are many variations of the kill shot, but they all have
the same end result: the ball stays so low after rebounding off the front wall
that to return it is virtually impossible. Also it may *roll out,* and when this occurs, the ball has no bounce as it rolls out on the floor after rebounding off the
front wall. The kill is the most spectacular of all shots; it leaves your opponent
helpless even when he sees it coming.

In the early learning stage, the kill shot is very difficult to execute consistently, but you should always attempt it if your position is correct and the
ball can be contacted low. The only time you should violate this rule is when
your opponent is in an excellent position to play your shot. Kill shots may be
played from different heights and from various positions on the court, but you
should concentrate on contacting the ball very low. This is the basic rule which
most beginners tend to disregard as they are usually too anxious to hit the ball
and so do not wait for it to drop sufficiently before attempting a kill shot. You
must have patience and wait for the ball to drop. You should attempt a kill
shot only when you have an easy play and are set for it. Remember that there
is some spot in the court where the ball will be in a position for the kill shot.

The simplest of the kill shots is the *straight kill* or the *front-wall kill.* You
can execute this shot from various positions—close to the front wall, in midcourt, near the back wall—depending upon the position of your opponent. As
the name implies most straight-kill shots come into and rebound in a straight
line from the front wall; the straight kill can be used effectively when driven
down a side wall or in a line away from where your opponent stands.

The most effective kill shot is the *corner* or *two-wall kill.* The ball should
first strike low on the side wall, very close to the front wall, and then strike the
front wall. After hitting low on the side wall, the ball rebounds in a downward
direction so that when it hits the front wall it is very close to the floor and has
a good possibility of rolling out. But if it does not, the ball still has a reduced
rebound off the front wall and floor, making it most difficult to return. For the
ball to hit the front wall first and then the side wall is also effective, but because
of the opposite spin generated, it will rebound higher off the floor area thus
give your opponent more time to play it. Also, in the corner kill when the ball
strikes the side wall first and then the front wall, it is traveling in a direction
away from your opponent, again making it more difficult to return. When the
ball hits the front wall first and then the side wall, the direction it travels is
more toward your opponent, which makes it easier to return.

To keep your kill shots low it is important that you assume a deep crouch
for the hit. If you are close to the front wall, keep your hand in an open cupped
position to enable you to get more force and spin on the ball so that it will drop
lower on contacting the walls. Quick movements are necessary in executing the
corner kill when you are positioned forward in the front court. In this shot,
rather than directly face the side wall, you should stand at approximately a
forty-five-degree angle to the side wall so that your forward hip is facing the
corner where you intend to hit the shot. In other words, you stand parallel to
the line of flight of the ball, that is, as you hit the ball a line drawn across both
toes should be parallel to the ball's line of flight.

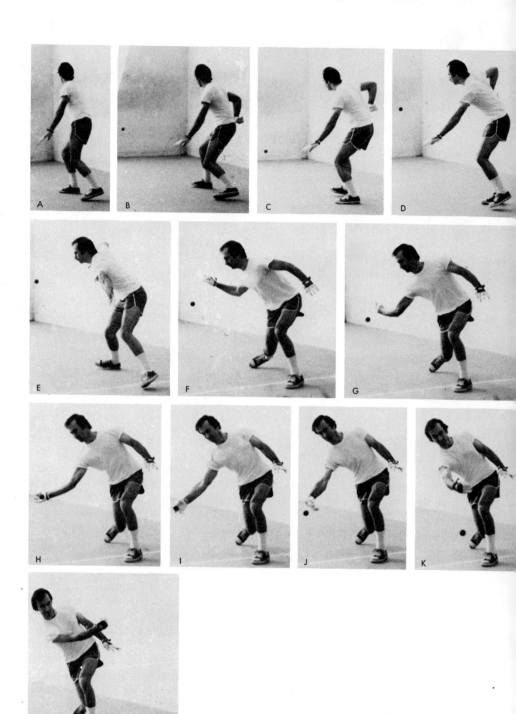

Fig. 3.16 Back Wall Play

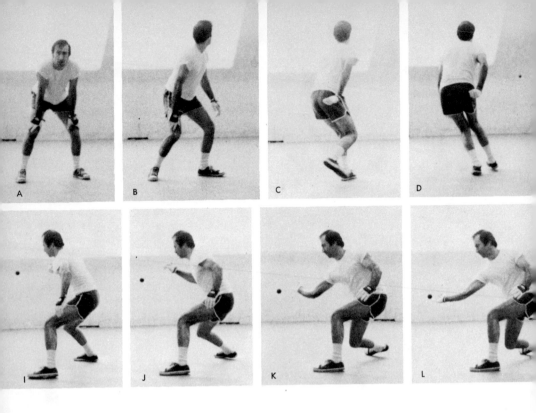

The kill shot is usually hit hard to help eliminate any chance of a return, but occasionally it may be hit easy. This is known as the *soft kill*. This shot should seldom be used and only when your opponent is in the back court and has little chance of returning the ball. The stroke is executed in exactly the same manner as the regular kill shot, except that the ball is hit easy and therefore dies soon after hitting the corner. Almost all kill shots should be used as offensive shots either to score a point or win the service from your opponent. A possible exception is the kill from the back wall which is usually a defensive shot, but it can result in an effective offensive hit (see fig. 5.4).

Back Wall Play   Playing the ball off the back wall will probably be one of the most difficult skills for you to master. Back-wall play requires considerable concentration and ability to position yourself correctly for the shot and not run or chase after the ball. It is essential that you keep looking at the ball while it is in flight and turn to face the backwall (figs. 3.16 and 3.17). In general, turn your body in the same direction that the ball is traveling (fig. 3.17, A-I) and be prepared to turn as you get ready for the hit so that you assume the all important position of facing the side wall. As the ball rebounds off the rear wall, you position yourself far enough away from the wall to allow the ball to drop to knee level or below before hitting it. In other words, you should move with the ball. As you travel with the ball, you can make the necessary calculations to arrive at the proper hitting spot and be in good position for the hit. Look at figures

Fig. 3.17   Back Wall Play

3.16 and 3.17. Notice how the player moves with the ball and positions himself for a kill or passing shot. The backswing movements begin as he turns around to follow the ball, and as the ball approaches, he steps forward with the foot nearest the front wall for forward weight shift and then rotates the body in exactly the same manner as previously described for hitting the ball.

In figure 3.17 you can see how the player actually squats somewhat to get low enough for the hit. It is not possible for him to execute the shot as demonstrated in figure 3.16 because of the placement of his left foot. When the foot is placed so that the toes point somewhat toward the front wall, the player is able to rotate the hips toward the front. However, when the toes are facing the side wall, hip rotation is impossible. When a ball coming out of a corner in the back court is played, it is almost impossible to place the forward foot so that the toes point forward because of the direction that the ball is traveling.

You must position yourself so that you are stable and can hit the ball; this is why the toes face the side wall. Although the squat position is poor because it does not allow for quick movements after the shot, the player has strong wrist flexion (wrist snap) and a long low follow-through which helps ensure that the ball stays low to the floor.

At times when a fast moving ball comes out of a rear corner, you may not have sufficient time to position yourself facing the side wall. In such cases you must rely upon body twist to carry your body around sufficiently to send the ball in a forward direction. Your body must turn during the hit, and when you complete the hit, your body should be completely turned so that you face the front wall.

The Passing Shot   Probably the most frequently used shot is the passing shot, commonly known as the workhorse of handball. The shot is relatively simple to execute as it can be hit with an overhead, sidearm, or underhand stroke and, as the name implies, is merely a straight shot driven past your opponent. The ball, which should strike the front wall first, is hit at such an angle that it carries past your opponent and beyond the short line, hitting either the side wall or the floor without reaching the rear wall. If the ball does reach the back wall, it should be so low that it cannot be returned before it bounces twice. A ball hitting several side walls expends its speeds and thereby gives your opponent more time to reach the ball.

To be most effective the passing shot should be hit very hard, a carom shot, so that it will have sufficient speed to go by your opponent before he can reach it. This shot should be used whenever your opponent is caught out of position. It is much more difficult to pass your opponent when he is in center court position or when he is positioned behind the service line. In these cases the ball should be hit so that it will remain very close to the side wall. This is a more difficult shot. Some of the best passing shots are hit with a bent arm overhand stroke, which is where the most power for this shot can be created (fig. 3.18). The power in this shot comes from strong shoulder girdle rotation and medial rotation in the shoulder joint (sequences E to G). The action is identical to that used in throwing a baseball or a football for a short distance. The bent arm overhand stroke is also the fastest shot because the ball travels in an almost level plane, though with some downward direction which helps increase the speed. The passing shot is used most often when your opponent is in the front court, close to the front wall.

The Ceiling Shot   The ceiling shot is another very effective shot that is relatively easy to execute. It is used far too little because its speed and direction are more difficult to control. It is a stroke that can be used both offensively and defensively. In this shot when you are in the center court, the ball should be hit upward with an overhand swing so that it hits the ceiling approximately two to three feet away from the front wall. The ball should contact the ceiling farther back from the front wall if you are hitting from the back court. When the ball

Fig. 3.18   The Bent Arm Overhand Stroke

hits the ceiling, it develops backspin, and when it hits the front wall, it drops sharply and rebounds very high off the floor. It is most difficult to return this rebound since the ball then will drop in the back court where it will probably hit low on the back wall and drop sharply to the floor. If the ball hits high on the rear wall, it once again drops sharply, making it more of a struggle to return. An advanced player is usually able to kill a ball coming off the back wall following a ceiling shot provided it is not hit into the corner close to the side wall and is at least above his knees on the rebound.

In order to execute this shot effectively the player must contact the ball high so that a full overhand or bent arm overhand stroke can be used (fig. 3.18). The ball should be hit with moderate or little force since a hard hit ball will

Fig. 3.19 The Ceiling Shot Using the Full Overhand Stroke

carry high onto the back wall, making a return possible. The main objective is to have the ball drop into the corner or hit so low on the back wall that it does not rebound.

To execute the shot well you must position yourself so that the ball will be high when it reaches you. When using the full overhand stroke, contact the ball with a straight arm directly overhead (fig. 3.19). You should lean to the rear sufficiently so that you can look up at the ball as it comes down toward you (sequence D). By keeping his left arm up, the player limits the amount of shoulder rotation, helping to ensure that the ball is not hit very hard. The hand remains cocked as elbow extension takes place, and as contact is made with the ball, the ball should roll from the palm to the fingertips, giving it additional backspin (sequences E to G). Wrist flexion assists in giving the ball backspin and is continued into the follow-through (sequence H). The ball will then rebound higher off the floor due to the greater spin.

In the bent arm ceiling shot the initial position (fig. 3.20, A) is almost identical to the overhand kill or passing shot (compare sequence A of fig. 3.20 with sequence E of fig. 3.18). The only difference is the lateral flexion and lean

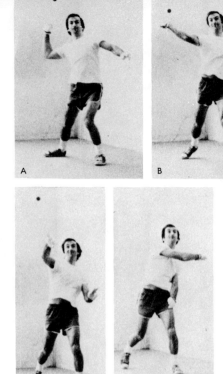

Fig. 3.20   The Ceiling Shot Using the Bent
Arm Stroke

of the trunk to the rear in the ceiling shot. Rather than use elbow joint extension, as in the full overhand stroke, the bent arm stroke utilizes medial rotation in the shoulder joint. Wrist action is almost the same except for a slight
amount of pronation. The spin imparted to the ball, however, is the same.

The ceiling shot is used to make your opponent move out of front court
position so that you can regain the advantage. As an offensive shot the ball is
hit off the ceiling at such an angle that when the ball rebounds off the front
wall and floor it stays very close to the side wall and/or falls into the rear corner.
This shot is especially difficult to return if it is hit into the corner where the
return involves using the weak arm in executing an overhand stroke.

The Lob Shot   In general if the ball is hit high, as in a lob or ceiling shot,
it should be returned with another high ceiling shot. The lob shot should be
used only when you want to gain the time necessary to take the offensive position. When the lob shot is executed, the ball should be hit easy, striking high
on the front wall. The hit should direct the ball to the rear corner so that the
rebound off the floor will give the ball just enough impetus to reach the rear
corner very close to the side wall. The same techniques used in the ceiling shot
can be employed to execute this shot.

The Fly Hit   At times you may find it necessary to volley the ball, that is,
hit it on the fly. This is a difficult shot to master, and you should use it only

Fig. 3.21 The Fly Hit, Hip High

when you have an easy opportunity, preferably when maintaining your position in front court. Hitting the ball on the fly should be attempted more often in doubles when you are in good front-court position and do not wish to go on the defensive by running into the back court. In singles you should attempt a volley when you can catch your opponent off guard with a quick passing shot. If a better shot can be executed by letting the ball bounce before hitting it, you should strive for this. If you try for too many volleys, you will invariably deny yourself a chance for a kill shot. A volley can be executed with the ball at the height which calls for a kill, passing, or ceiling shot. In all fly ball hits you should go through the same motions as described for execution of other shots, but greater concentration is needed to help ensure proper timing (figs. 3.21 and 3.22).

Fig. 3.22 The Fly Hit, Shoulder High

It is interesting to note that the players shown in figures 3.21 and 3.22 have a cupped hand and slightly spread-apart fingers, which is indicative of a relaxed hand and little wrist action. Both players have good forward weight shift and very stable position during the hit. The performer in figure 3.22 continues his weight shift in the follow-through, a move that allows him to come completely around and to need take only one step to be back in the ready position. The performer in figure 3.21 finishes his follow-through in what is basically the hitting position. He is, however, facing the front wall, and he will need a fraction of a second longer to assume the ready position or to begin movement to another spot. For this player this is not a detriment because he has great speed and very quick movements.

Do not attempt to volley when you are off balance or when you have to overstretch or lunge for the ball. Also, you may find that there is insufficient time to execute all the necessary body movements. The ball travels toward you will great speed; consequently, you need meet it with only firm forward motion in order to return it with ample force.

The Pickup   When in front-court position and the ball is hit at you hard, fairly low, and bounces right at your feet, you should immediately prepare for a *pickup* (hitting the ball immediately as it rebounds off the floor). You should remain facing the front wall and use an underhand stroke, keeping the arm straight and the wrist firm. Use the sidearm-underhand stroke when you have to move to the side to get to the ball. It is very important that you keep your eyes constantly focused on the ball during flight and while making the hit, for the slightest deviation is sufficient to throw your swing off. As a result the hit will usually be weak or you will miss it altogether.

Once you become a better player, you will sometimes make a good hit even though you do not look at the ball during contact. This is due to the fact that your swing is grooved in. Your actions have become automatic, and you can complete the swing without deep concentration on the ball during the contact phase. An example of this action is shown in figure 3.23. By sequence E it is apparent that the performer is no longer looking at the ball, but he executes a good hit as the ball comes up off the floor (sequence G). However, he contacts the ball too far out in front and as a consequence returns it high to the front wall. Thus the shot is defensive, rather than offensive.

The pickup is used many times as a defensive shot whose main purpose is merely to return the ball to the front wall—a necessary maneuver especially when the player is off-balance. When the pickup is used as an offensive shot, the ball is hit with the intent of making low placement on the front wall or in a corner. The shot is also used effectively as a passing shot when your opponent is out of position.

The Wall Hugger Shot   Many times in a game situation you will find that the ball is traveling right next to the side wall, hugging the wall, and must be returned from this close wall position. In order to hit the ball you should slide the hand alongside the wall. The little-finger side of the hand should be in contact with the wall. Do not take a full swing or swing so that the fingers hit the wall because there is a good chance that the fingers will be severely injured.

Because you cannot take a full swing at the ball, you must utilize tremendous wrist action to impart force to the ball. The player shown in figure 3.24 exhibits excellent wrist action (sequences E to H). To add additional power to the hit he rotates the shoulder girdle somewhat prior to contact (sequences C-E). To execute the shot well you must maintain intense concentration on the ball.

ADDITIONAL HINTS

It is essential that you master the fundamental elements of the swing before you can expect to execute successfully the various serves and shots which comprise the sport of four-wall handball. Always think immediately of turning your body so that you will face the side wall to be in a position to take a full, smooth swing. Think in terms of a split body. If the ball approaches on your left, turn to use your left hand, and if the ball approaches on the right side, move to use your right hand. In executing your shots do not move in a direction to favor one arm over the other.

During the swing think of shifting the weight forward, rotating the trunk and shoulders into the shot as well as bringing the arm through its full range of motion. Keep your eyes on the ball throughout the swing and completion of the hit in order to gain accuracy in direction. Contact the ball with a slightly cupped hand at the junction of the palm and fingers and get the feel of snapping the wrist in the throwing, slinging motion of the hit. Remember, the elbow leads in almost all strokes.

You must keep these essentials in mind during the execution of the various shots which utilize the underhand, sidearm, and overhand strokes or combina-

Fig. 3.23   The Pickup

tion of these strokes. Learn to react immediately to a situation with a definite stroke. In a game situation begin to think about which shot will be most advantageous. In other words, use strategy: plan ahead rather than just hit the ball and hope it will score a point. Always try to hit the ball away from your opponent. Think of the shots that will force your opponent out of position—including the kill, passing, and ceiling shots. Be in the right place at the right time. Do not jeopardize your position by being on one side or the other, thereby allowing your opponent to execute a passing shot or any other equally effective shot. Always get ready prior to the hit if you hope to have perfect or near perfect execution of the return shot. As mastery of these basic strokes and shots is developed, you will then be ready to go on to the more advanced shots which are very necessary for playing top-level handball.

Fig. 3.24 The Wall Hugger Shot

Improving your game

4

Proper physical conditioning can speed up learning and development. General exercises which develop muscular strength and endurance, agility, speed, flexibility, circulatory and respiratory endurance, and neuromuscular coordination are helpful in producing the all-around physical capabilities necessary to play handball well. Once you acquire these necessary requisites, you will receive greater satisfaction and enjoyment from playing the game. Naturally your enthusiasm for handball will increase as you find you (1) have greater power in your serves and shots, (2) can move faster to reach the ball, (3) can change direction and position yourself for a shot quickly, (4) have increasing amounts of energy which make it possible for you to play longer and at a higher level, (5) have the ability to make quick and accurate decisions, and (6) are able to evaluate various playing situations correctly and can carry out your plans. You should remember that the difference between winning and losing is many times accounted for by differences in fitness.

PHYSICAL CONDITIONING

General physical conditioning is especially important during the early learning stages. Later after you can play fairly well (in about six to twelve months, depending upon how much you practice and play), you will not need to perform a wide range of conditioning exercises. Merely playing the game will be adequate to maintain fitness for your level of play. However, if you desire to become a better performer—to the point of becoming a top tournament player—you will need additional fitness work. In other words, you have to develop a level of fitness (in all the physical qualities required) commensurate with the level at which you want to play. Your level of physical preparation determines your playing level!

The reasons should be obvious. For example, if you want to hit a particular shot such as a low, hard underhand-sidearm shot, you must have the necessary strength, power, flexibility, and agility to execute the hit. You should not keep trying to learn a difficult shot if you do not have the necessary physical capabilities. Not only will it be a waste of time, but it will also be very frustrating. Failure to learn particular shots and strokes because of inadequate development of the necessary physical qualities is the main reason why many people give up trying to learn or master a new sport. Do not let this happen to you. Being physically prepared enables you to learn effectively and in addition to experience greater vitality and well-being in your normal everyday activities.

Before undertaking a conditioning program and/or playing handball, you should have a thorough medical examination. Only in this way can you be sure that the activities in which you want to participate will not be detrimental or damaging.

In order for your physical conditioning program to be successful, you should keep foremost in your mind the following general principles of training. First, your training work must be done on a regular basis. If it is performed in a haphazard manner, training will be of little, if any, value. Training should take place a minimum of three times per week on alternate days. Exercises for small muscle groups (such as squeezing a rubber ball to strengthen the finger flexors and wrist) can be performed daily. Also, flexibility exercises should be done daily or twice daily. Heavy load or resistance exercises should be handled only two to three times per week. Included are such exercises as leg squats involving large muscles (quadriceps muscle group on the front side of the thigh).

Secondly, exercise must be progressive. Doing exercises with the same number of repetitions and/or amounts of resistance for more than two or three weeks will not result in additional development of any physical quality. The same exercise only helps to maintain an achieved level, and does not increase development. In general, you should increase the load every week or so. When you begin from a relatively low level of physical preparation, you can increase the load substantially and quite rapidly. When you have attained a high level of physical preparation, increase should be smaller and less frequent.

Third, the physical conditioning program must be carried out for at least several months, if not more. A crash course in physical preparation is impossible. This concept has been perpetuated by many coaches who erroneously believe that it is possible to get players in shape in two weeks. It has been well documented that a minimum of at least eight weeks is necessary before substantial physiological changes in the body take place. Most early improvement in physical condition is due to the learning process, that is, to developing the skills needed to perform the exercise. Therefore, it is important that you not expect too much too soon. Be patient. After the minimum two or three months have passed, you will be well on your way to long-lasting physical preparation.

The fourth principle to keep in mind is that skill learning (technique) and physical conditioning must be done together. For example, if conditioning work is performed three days a week, work on skill and/or game play should be done on the other three or four days. If you practice handball more than three times per week (which you should if you hope to improve your game rapidly), you should always do the conditioning work after handball practice. When learning new skills or just working on technique, you must be alert and not fatigued. Also when new skills are being learned, short, frequent practice sessions are most advantageous. When you become a better player, sessions on technique can be longer and more intense, usually one or more hours, and less frequent, one or two times per week.

Fifth, you must realize that a training program is only as good as the person executing the prescribed workouts. Training is a very personal matter. If you train as required, you will reap the benefits. If you do not you will join many people who end by wasting their time "practicing" and developing a negative attitude because of slow and/or poor learning (improvement). As an aid in maintaining your conditioning program, you should keep a diary of your daily and/or weekly workouts. Only in this way will you be able to evaluate your progress objectively. A record of all conditioning, technique, and playing sessions will be of great value to you, especially if you aspire to be a top player. By looking over your records you will be able to determine both the strong and weak points in your program in relation to the results of your game play.

The actual training program should consist of various localized (limited to specific areas of the body) exercises as well as of total body activities. Localized exercises are used essentially for the development of muscular strength and endurance, for flexibility (range of motion), and in some cases for improvement of technique. Total body activities (for example, running) are for the development of cardiovascular endurance, muscular endurance, agility, speed of movement, and technique.

LOCALIZED EXERCISES

For the development of strength, you should use heavy resistance exercises, with few repetitions. For example, if the most you can lift in a particular exercise is 200 pounds (91 kilograms) you should exercise with approximately 160 to 190 pounds (73 to 86 kilograms), using two to eight repetitions. The exercise should be done slowly through a complete range of motion. Many times by going through a complete range of motion, you can increase flexibility at the same time you develop strength.

If your prime objective is muscular endurance, you should perform many repetitions using little resistance (or only body weight, as the case may be). For example, if you use the same exercise as for strength development, but execute 25 to 100 repetitions, with no added resistance (or with 5 to 50 additional pounds), you can develop muscular endurance.

Generally, the game of handball requires much more muscular endurance than pure strength and therefore your workout should be directed toward endurance. No set number of repetitions or amount of resistance can be recommended here. Such decisions depend not only upon your initial physical condition, but also upon your level of aspiration.

To develop flexibility use a slow sretch method. For example, if you are working for greater flexibility in the hip joint so that you can take longer steps or get lower for a shot, you do the hamstring stretch in a sitting position as follows: Keep the legs straight (knees locked) and try to touch your toes with your hands by slowly stretching forward (fig. 4.1). Relax the body completely and

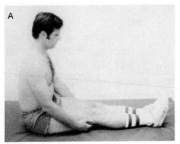

Fig. 4.1   The Hamstring Stretch

continue trying to stretch the hands to the toes. Do the exercise for approximately one minute (five to eight tries). After you develop enough flexibility to execute all movements and shots effectively, you need not continue flexibility work—provided that you continue to play three to five times per week on a regular basis. Game playing will maintain flexibility, although you should do considerable stretching prior to beginning play.

Technique can be enhanced by doing specialized local exercises. In this case, do not perform the complete action, but only the portion of the action in one or two joints as needed. Usually such technique work is done in conjunction with an exercise for the development of strength or endurance. An example of this is an exercise involving only wrist action as described for hitting a particular shot (see fig. 4.7).

Some of the best exercises for developing muscular strength and endurance of the major muscles involved in arm movement are pull-ups (chin-ups) with palms toward you and away from you, push-ups with the elbows perpendicular to the body (fig. 4.2), bent arm (forearm) pullovers (fig. 4.3), and flying motions in which arm movement alternates as the arms are crossed (fig. 4.4). These four exercises aid the power phase of the underhand, sidearm, and overhand strokes.

To improve wrist action for hitting, perform the following exercises. Wrist curls with the palm up and the palm down. An example of this exercise with the palm up is shown in figure 4.5. Dumbbells can also be used in this exercise instead of barbells. Wrist adduction and abduction done with a dumbbell loaded at one end are shown in figure 4.6. To perform adduction hold the dumbbell behind you. Hand supination and pronation, which are so important for executing hops and putting spin on the ball, should be executed with a dumbbell. With flexion in the elbow joint, the forearm horizontal, and the hand holding

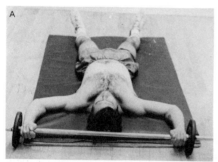

Fig. 4.2   The Push-Up

Fig. 4.3   The Bent Arm Pullover

 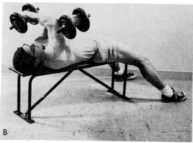

Fig. 4.4   Flying Motion (Courtesy of Gene O'Connell and Wm. C. Brown Company Publishers)

Do you know how to space the practice of your conditioning exercise? How often should you exercise small muscle groups? How often should you work on flexibility? How often is it advisable to handle heavy resistance exercises?

Fig. 4.5 The Wrist Curl

Fig. 4.6 Wrist Abduction (Courtesy of Gene O'Connell and Wm. C. Brown Company Publishers)

the dumbbell, turn the hand first palm up and then palm down. This exercise can be done from the same position as for the wrist curl, but with a dumbbell in one hand.

To put some of the previous moves together (and to add elbow joint flexion which is also very important for putting spin on the ball) do the Zottman curl (fig. 4.7). In this exercise you curl the weight, pronate the hand, and then lower it. Then reverse the curl to the chest, supinate the hand, and lower it.

To develop the muscles most involved in rotation of the shoulder girdle (getting your shoulders and upper body into the hit) perform the following exercises: (1) sit-ups (curl-ups) with a twist, keeping the knees bent and alternating right-and-left twists as you curl up (fig. 4.8); (2) twists in bent-over position, using barbells weighted at one or both ends placed on the shoulders with the hands spread wide (fig. 4.9) as you try to touch the weighted end of each bar-

Fig. 4.7   The Zottman Curl (Courtesy of Gene O'Connell and Wm. C. Brown Company Publishers)

Fig. 4.8   The Sit-Up with the Twist

Fig. 4.9   The Bent Over Twist

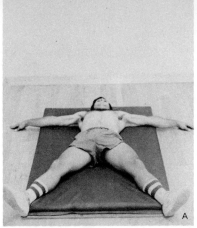

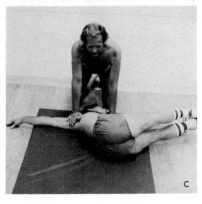

Fig. 4.10 The Twisting Leg Raises; **B,** Single Leg; **C,** Double Leg

bell to the opposite foot; (3) single- and/or double-twist leg raises from the supine position so that the toes touch the opposite hand while the shoulders are kept in contact with the floor (fig. 4.10); and (4) back raises with half-twist (fig. 4.11).

In order to execute short, fast movements you must have strong legs. The muscles responsible for ankle, knee, and hip action must be capable of very

Fig. 4.11 The Back Raise with Half Twist

Fig. 4.12   The Heel Raise (Courtesy of
Wm. C. Brown Company Publishers)

quick, powerful **contractions. To prepare** these muscles initially you must develop their strength. The best exercises are the heel raise (fig. 4.12) for the ankle joint, the leg squat (fig. 4.13) for the knee joint, and the lateral leg lift for
the hip joint.

As the muscles involved in these joint actions become stronger, you should
begin to do forward and side lunges (fig. 4.14) and various kinds of depth

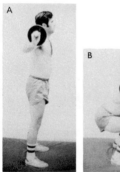

Fig. 4.13   The Leg Squat (Half Squat)

jumps. Included are shallow and deep single and double leg hops (fig. 4.15),
squat jumps, jumps over objects of various heights, jumps from a bench in
which you rebound immediately after hitting the ground, long and short stride
jumps for short distances, and other similar activities. The side jump (fig. 4.16)
is also very good because it comes very close to movements used in handball
play, especially for changing directions.

All the activities just discussed aid in making quick starts, in accelerating,
and in getting the body into the hit. Variations of some of these activities such
as executing side, front, and rear cutting movements while keeping the eyes
fixed on a target also improve agility. Similar activities such as side running be-

Fig. 4.14   The Forward and Side Lunge

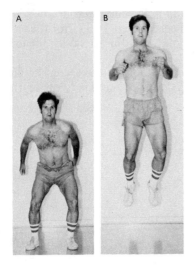

Fig. 4.15   The Double Leg Hop (Jump)

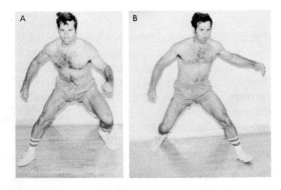

Fig. 4.16   The Side Jump

tween the side walls (touching the floor at the junction of the side wall) for time, develop speed of movement along with agility. Many different activities and/or drills can be done to develop the various physical qualities. The activities just described are by no means the only ones. A professional physical educator can provide further information.

TOTAL BODY ACTIVITIES

Some of the activities such as the depth jumps and cutting and running movements can be considered total body activities, depending upon speed of execution, duration of the exercise, and amount of rest in between exercises. When rest between exercises is shortened and execution is speeded up, these exercises become anaerobic (performed in the absence of oxygen), which is beneficial because most handball play requires anaerobic activity. To supplement these exercises you should do short sprints (10 to 40 meters) at maximum speed, with 5 to 15 seconds of rest between repetitions.

Your circulatory and respiratory endurance should be fairly strong before you undertake sprinting exercises. To develop this quality you must run long distances (2 to 10 kilometers) at a moderate pace—pulse rate between 150 and 160 beats per minute. Running of this nature should be done at the end of a workout, never prior to a practice or conditioning session or to game play. If you follow this plan, you will derive maximum benefits from your efforts: effective learning, better playing skill, and less fatigue, along with strengthened aerobic capabilities.

As you start your physical conditioning program, you will soon discover your weak areas and your strong areas. In planning your workouts you should then make sure that the weak areas receive the necessary attention. This is the only sure way to experience effective improvement and avoid exercises for physical qualities already on a high level. Your time is important, and you should make the most of each training session. Also, it is not necessary to do every exercise described at every training session. All are mentioned to provide variety for your program and to make your practice sessions more enjoyable and, in the end, more productive.

THE WARM-UP

Before beginning to play a game you should make sure that you are well warmed up and have practiced the various hitting coordinations. This helps prevent injury to the muscles and allows you to start your game at a high level. You should not begin to play a game until you feel loose and can hit the ball well, even if your opponent is urging you to a quick start. To begin your warm-up, start with calisthenics designed to stretch the muscles and connective tissue around all the joints. Include such exercises as arm circles, side stretching, deep knee bends, front and side splits, trunk bending and twisting, and running in place. You should then slowly begin throwing the ball with underhand, side-arm, and overhand movements, using both arms.

After you have been playing the game for a period of time and have some mastery of the various shots, you should increase your warm-up time and make it more specific. Throw for special shots such as throwing the ball to the back corners with a return hit to the front wall, throwing against the back wall for a straight kill shot, hitting straight and corner kill shots from a position in front court, hitting fly balls, hitting ceiling shots, and executing different serves.

The warm-up should be varied, especially if you have trouble with a particular shot or if you need to stretch certain muscles more. Once warmed up, you should be ready to play.

TRAINING PRACTICE

The key to a strong game is practice. Practice constantly, repeating the strokes and shots until you are able to perform them automatically. Many people seem to equate practice with drudgery, but remember that there are many ways to practice which are both interesting and challenging. Practice, however, should be performed diligently with maximum effort, for there is no other way for learning and development to take place.

When you practice it is important to know what your practice is for and how to perform the skill. You should keep in mind the specific stroke or shot that you want to improve or learn and direct your practice toward this end. Almost every stroke or shot can be practiced either individually or with a partner by merely throwing the ball in a way that duplicates situations that arise during a regular game.

In the very first stages of learning it is worthwhile to practice the basic strokes without regard to where the ball goes. If you have trouble integrating the body parts in the swing, you should then practice the stroke without the ball. To develop the basic stroke and eye-hand coordination, it is advantageous to position yourself facing the side wall; bounce the ball to the desired position and height and then execute the stroke being worked on. After success with this practice, throw the ball to the front wall so that it rebounds to the desired spot and once again go through the same action. Once you have mastered the stroke, assume a ready position, throw the ball to the front wall, turn for correct hitting position, and repeat the stroke. Then practice by throwing the ball short and/or long from the ready position so that you must move up or back to get into position before repeating the entire swing.

Practice of this nature is progressive. You add a new element to those already learned each time you practice. As you begin to play games, you will very soon discover your weaknesses, and your practice should then be directed to correct these weaknesses, one at a time. Remember that a good player will always play to your weaknesses. If he has good placements, you may find that your greatest weakness is the nonpreferred arm, and therefore specific attention should be directed toward its improvement. One of the best ways to start is to get the feel of throwing the ball with the nonpreferred hand in underhand, side-arm, and overhand motions. As total body coordination is developed, you should begin to hit the ball in the progressive manner already described. In the beginning and later stages at least three-fourths of your practice time should be spent working with the nonpreferred arm until it can function as effectively as the other arm.

To practice the various shots when working alone you should throw the ball in a manner to imitate the effect you desire. For example, to practice the back wall shot, stand facing the back wall and throw the ball against the wall so that it rebounds to you at various heights in order to practice returning the ball with a kill or a passing shot. To practice back wall corner shots do the same thing: throw the ball either on a fly or on a bounce into a corner and then return the ball with different shots in different directions. As you become more proficient, throw the ball hard against the front wall so that it will rebound in the back corner for the same desired effect.

Before attempting the ceiling shot you should first throw many ceiling balls from the back court to acquaint yourself with the different angles of rebound which come from varying speeds. You should then throw the ball easy and high on the front wall so that it will rebound high in the back court where you are positioned and then execute the ceiling shot. This exercise can be alternated with back wall play; then you can either hit the ball for a ceiling shot or let it rebound off the rear wall and attempt a kill shot.

For practice of kill shots you should position yourself in front center court or closer and work on hitting a kill both from a dropped ball and on a rebound from the front wall. For corner kills assume the same court position, but hit for the corners, trying to hit the side wall first. This should be done from a straight throw to the front wall and from a throw into the corner as you progress. As your proficiency in killing the ball from a position close to the front wall increases, you should gradually increase the distance from the front wall. Similar situations can be set up for practice of other shots. After skill is developed in the basic strokes and shots, practice time should be devoted to development of fast footwork and ability to change directions quickly while moving. Trying to maintain a rally from center court position is a very effective drill for practice of these elements. Major concern should be given to proper position and movement rather than to how effectively you hit the ball. As footwork is developed, more attention can then be directed to the execution of shots.

Serves should be practiced individually, and attention should be focused on where the ball hits the front wall, where the ball rebounds, and what the effect is. You should look to see where the ball goes so that in a game situation you will know where the ball is and not have to look immediately back after executing a desired shot. In all of these practices both arms should be used.

When you practice with another person, the same drills can be executed. One player sets the ball up and the other tries for the return. This arrangement can be very beneficial if the one setting up the shots can also detect errors and point them out to you. In this way any tendency to pick up bad habits will be diminished and learning will be enhanced. You should have expert instruction in the basic skills as well as have your mistakes pointed out and corrected.

It is very beneficial to practice drills for placements and passing shots. Have the receiver stand in front of you in center court position with the ball. Let him throw the ball to the front wall so that it rebounds to you; then you try to pass him on either side. Analogous setups can be arranged to practice kill, ceiling, and lob shots. As proficiency increases, the service and return can be practiced by two players. The server announces a shot, and you prepare for it with a specific return. In time this practice can be carried on without advance notice of the shot. You can also play out the point after a legal serve and service return.

In another variation the receiver assumes the ready position in center court and his partner throws the ball, simulating a particular shot. The receiver then tries to return the ball. The point may be played out if desired. If both of you have weak left arms, play a game using only the left arm for all serves and most shots. Right-handed hits should be taken only when the ball is close to the right side wall. This is probably the best practice to force yourself to use the weak arm and speed its development.

Practice should approximate the game situation as closely as possible. Many other variations can be used as development of the basic fundamentals continues. For example, to practice the volley, kill, and passing shots, rally with a multitude of strokes, using a side wall as the front wall and the opposite side wall as the back wall. Because of the shorter distance thus provided, the play is very fast, which helps develop your reaction time. Very important in all practice is to analyze what you do so that you can determine if you are utilizing all the principles of proper stroking and hitting. If you are cognizant of what you are doing, you will be able to correct yourself. This is an important step toward continuous improvement, especially when your instructor is not present. Equally important is to be able to develop the ability to think ahead—to determine the possible offensive and/or defensive shots that can be used and to anticipate the shots that may be hit to you in various situations. In the more advanced stages it is important that you be able to analyze your game in order to determine your weaknesses and to analyze your opponent's game to determine his strong and weak points so that you can build your game accordingly.

COMPETITION

In order to improve steadily and keep your game on a high level, you should play as much as possible. With sufficient playing you will be able to maintain proper timing and keep skills at maximum peak. Playing in many tournaments is also very important even if you do not aspire to become a class A player. In tournament play you must play your best game; you are forced to try for precise placements and execution of the various shots. Of at least equal importance is the fact that during tournament play you have an opportunity to learn from your opponent, especially if he is a better player and has some strokes or shots that you feel would be effective in your game. This is one of the reasons why you always should try to play with someone who is more skilled since you can pick up many pointers if you are alert and have learned to analyze.

Have you investigated to find out where handball courts are in your community? whether tournaments are sponsored? Which category of tournament play is open to you as a beginning or intermediate player?

You can also gain much from watching top-level performers in various tournaments. When you are a spectator, you are more relaxed and can more readily follow the play. You can observe the shots used most often by the better players and also note when they are used. You can pick up many new ideas, especially strategy and finer points of play, from top competitors. If the information is applicable, incorporate it into your game so that you constantly improve and strengthen your game.

Tournaments are not just for champions. Many levels of tournament play are available in areas where handball is played. Tournaments are held quite often by athletic clubs, YMCAs, recreation departments, colleges, and universities. If you live in an area where there are several handball centers, you can probably find a tournamnt every month or so. There are usually three categories of play in most tournaments: class A for advanced players, class B for intermediate to advanced players, and class C for beginning to intermediate players. If it is a large recognized tournament, and you win in either class C or B, you must then play in the next higher bracket. In this way all players have a chance to continue to advance, but yet play on a level consistent with their ability. For national tournament play you should be a class A player and a very good one at that.

Most tournaments are held on weekends so that everyone has a chance to play, even players who work or attend school during the week. Occasionally you may find a local club tournament held in the evenings. If it is a large tournament, it will usually include both singles and doubles. To learn of these tournaments you should keep in touch with your local club or center where handball is played.

Information about regional and national tournaments as well as local news is provided by Ace, a national magazine devoted to handball. Included in this magazine are articles on various aspects of handball, pertinent information on playing the game, and results of handball tournaments throughout the country. This magazine is considered a player's magazine, individual subscriptions can be obtained by writing to the United States Handball Association Magazine, 4101 Dempster Street, Skokie, Illinois.

The United States Handball Association (USHA) holds a number of national handball tournaments throughout the year and conducts many exhibition tours throughout the country. USHA is mainly responsible for the national tournament and aids also in governing the various regional competitions. Some of the finest tournaments throughout the country are conducted by the many private athletic clubs and YMCAs in almost all large cities. There are many invitational meets with other clubs throughout the year, and everyone who holds membership is eligible to play. These and other clubs have played a major role in maintaining and fostering the growth of handball for many years.

KEY REMINDERS

Following are some of the important points that you should remember—specific reminders and hints for playing a better game. These reminders are based on the more common errors committed by beginning players. If you keep these points constantly in mind, you will also keep your mistakes to a minimum and be able to play your best game.

1. In practice and during warm-up do a great deal of throwing, especially with the weaker arm.
2. Keep your eye on the ball as you prepare to hit it and while you are hitting it.
3. Step into the ball and take a full swing.
4. Split your body in half. If the ball approaches on the left side, take it with the left hand. If it comes to the right side, use the right arm. Use both hands.
5. In back wall play, swing in the direction that the ball travels when it rebounds off the back wall.
6. If the ball is high, hit it high; if the ball is low, hit it low.
7. Learn the kill shot and keep trying it. However, do not kill every shot. Mix your shots.
8. Let the ball come to you; do not rush your shots.
9. Aim for a specific spot on the wall; do not just hit and hope. Make a mental picture of the path the ball will take, especially on returns.
10. Use the side walls and ceiling as much as possible in hits.
11. Maintain center court position before and after a shot.
12. In doubles as soon as your partner's serve passes the short line, get into position to hit the return shot by your opponents. Never be caught in a position with your back against the wall unable to swing at the ball.
13. Remember that speed is a great asset, but control wins more games.
14. Develop effective serves; each service should be difficult to return. When in doubt, serve to the corners and put spin on the ball.
15. Always be ready; think ahead, anticipate.
16. Try all shots. Practice them and do not be afraid that you will not be successful.

Better players master these techniques

5

GENERAL CHARACTERISTICS

A few general characteristics immediately distinguish the better player. He executes his shots efficiently and the results are effective. His movements are smooth, well-coordinated, and automatic. He anticipates the play and reacts immediately to quickly changing situations. Not only is his footwork automatic, but he is also almost always in the right position to execute his shots. Instinctively he turns his body to face the side wall, shifts his weights into the shot, strokes, anticipates his opponent's hit, plans his own response, and moves to his ready position. All these decisions and actions appear to be automatic for the better player; they occur as soon as he sees the ball coming off the front wall and often well before. The ability to anticipate, however, is at least partly the result of experience. Thinking in advance not only allows the good player to put pressure on this opponent, but also gives him the advantage of having time to conserve his energy between shots.

ADVANCED SHOTS AND STROKES

The better player is able to get into proper position for each shot because he follows the ball longer; consequently he has a good idea where the ball will rebound and so can prepare for it. On all shots you should follow the ball until it is about to be hit (provided that you are wearing eye guards and/or you keep an arm in front of your eyes to block the ball when it is hit directly at you). Though you do not watch the actual hit, you should take notice of your opponent's body position in relation to the ball so that you can calculate where and with which shot the ball will be hit. By drawing an imaginary line across the toes of both feet when the receiver is ready to hit the ball, you can determine the direction in which your opponent aims. You also can take notice of his general stance: if he is in a deep crouch, look for a low shot; if on a high bounce he dips his rear shoulder, prepare yourself for a ceiling shot; if he is standing fairly straight, he probably plans a passing shot. Once you have read your opponent's intention, make no anticipatory move until the actual swing is begun, for your opponent will change his shot or direction very quickly if he sees you move in anticipation of his shot.

The Wrist Snap

In situations requiring immediate action, you should use only the wrist snap with little or no body action; this shot should be used only as a last resort when the ball is in tight and you have no chance to employ a more effective shot. The wrist snap requires fast, vigorous contraction of the hand flexors in order to impart sufficient power and speed to the ball.

In executing almost all other shots you should use greater wrist action in order to impart more force and/or spin to the ball. However, when using great wrist snap you must make contact with the ball farther to the rear, that is, more toward the rear foot. If you make contact with the ball off your forward foot and add wrist flexion, you will direct the ball up toward the ceiling (if you use an underhand stroke), to the left if you use a sidearm stroke, and downward if you use an overhead stroke. A combination of where the ball is contacted in relation to the body and the amount of wrist action used determine the direction of flight of the ball. The correct combination will come with trial and error.

The Hop

A very effective shot used by advanced players is the *hop*, known also as a hook, reverse hop, or natural hop. In a hop, as the name implies, the ball upon hitting the floor from the front wall hops to either the right or left. In order to produce a hop it is necessary to place spin or English on the ball. The ball should strike the front wall at an angle that will cause it to rebound directly to the floor, at the receiver's feet. The spin then causes the ball to hop to one side or the other. The ball should not hit the side wall or back wall after hopping from the floor because it will lose its spin and result in an easy setup.

When serving a hop shot to break to the left (the natural hop), you should stand a little to the right of center in the service zone, facing the right side wall. The stroke is usually made in practically the same manner as the power serve (compare fig. 5.1 with fig. 3.10), but can be modified (fig. 5.2). The major difference between the power serve and the natural hop is supination of the hitting hand before and during the contact phase when the hop is executed. In other words, move the hand so that the palm of the hand turns toward the ceiling and right side wall. As your cupped hand contacts the ball, it rolls across your palm and leaves from the index finger and thumb. Your elbow remains close to the body throughout the hit and the hand is sliced across and under the ball, as in a chopping action. This cutting action on the ball creates much

Fig. 5.1   The Natural Hop

side spin, or clockwise spin on a horizontal axis when viewed from behind. If the ball has clockwise spin on a vertical axis, it will break sharply to the left when rebounding from the front wall. The ball must spin on a horizontal axis. The spin does not affect the ball as it hits the wall, but causes it to hop to the left as it strikes the floor. To achieve the most effective hop, it is important to hit the ball so that it travels and rebounds parallel with the floor. The ball should hit the front wall a little to the left of center so that it rebounds sufficiently far from the side wall so that it does not strike the wall after hopping. To return the hop, try to play it on the rebound off the hop; if you cannot do this, probably no other play is possible.

Examination of figures 5.1 and 5.2 reveals how both performers execute an effective natural hop. Each has good weight shift (sequences A and A), but the player shown in figure 5.1 may have more power because of greater hip and shoulder rotation prior to contact with the ball. This is not always an asset since

Fig. 5.2 The Modified Natural Hop

the hop can be executed very effectively with a relatively slow swing. What happens to the ball during contact is the key, not how hard the ball is hit. A possible reason why the performer in figure 5.1 utilizes greater power is that as he executes the hop his action practically duplicates the action in a power serve. He also supinates the hand very early (sequence C) and utilizes a chopping action in contacting the ball. The performer in figure 5.2 makes contact with the ball with a slightly supinated hand. Additional supination of the hand occurs during contact to impart the necessary spin to the ball.

The ball leaves the hand in approximately the same manner for both performers (fig. 5.1, F and fig. 5.2, E). Notice how after leaving the hand the ball appears to be coming straight at you. This is due to the fact that the hand action is very fast and actually gets ahead of the ball as the ball leaves the fingers. Compare this with other hits to see that the ball does not merely rebound off the hand.

For a less drastic hop to the left, but an equally effective service, stand on the left side of the service zone close to the left side wall. Use the same stroke in hitting the ball but direct the hit to the front wall at a greater angle so that the ball rebounds toward the right corner. When the ball hits the floor, instead of going into the side wall as it appears to be going, it hops slightly to the left as it strikes the floor and remains close to the side wall until it drops into the corner.

To produce a right or reverse hop (fig. 5.3) use a spin opposite to that for a left hop. To do this you should pronate the hand. In other words turn the hand so that the palm turns toward the body and the floor and make contact with the ball when it is farther away from your body. Your should hit the ball on the outside, and as contact with the ball is made, wrap your hand around the ball in an up-and-over motion. After initial contact is made, the ball should be allowed to roll across the fingers and palm of your hand, leaving from off the tips of the middle fingers. As the ball rolls across your hand and fingers, counterclockwise spin is imparted to the ball on an almost horizontal axis (when viewed from the rear), which in turn causes the ball to bounce sharply to the right when it hits the floor after rebounding off the front wall.

The same basic serves can be achieved with a right hop as with a left hop by reversing the initial starting positions. For the straight right hop serve you should stand a little to the left of center in the service zone and hit the ball low and a little to the right of center on the front wall. For the corner shot you should stand on the right side of the service lane and hit the ball left of center on the front wall so that it goes toward the left corner. As the ball rebounds from the floor, it hops slightly to the right and travels almost parallel to the side wall.

You should use the same body motion for both the left and right hops in order to prevent your opponent from knowing which hop is coming. You should perfect both hops; otherwise your opponent will soon expect only one hop and be able to prepare himself for it. It is not essential to hit the ball very hard in order to achieve a sharp breaking hop because perfect timing and contact are more important in imparting the necessary spin. The longer the hand remains in contact with the ball, the greater is the spin, provided that the hand action is correct.

Hops are a valuable asset to both your serves and passing shots. The receiver who is chasing or charging a shot will usually be thrown off balance when the ball takes a sharp hop to one side. Sharply breaking hops, however, require very vigorous movement of the forearm; therefore it is very important that you be sufficiently warmed up and loose before attempting these shots. They require good muscular development also.

The Kill Shot

One of the most spectacular skills of the top player is the kill shot, which he can execute from any place on the court (fig. 5.4). A top player uses any stroke or combination of strokes when executing the kill shot, although the sidearm is favored. The top player uses the kill shot often, but only because he has the shot well developed and is confident that his shot will be effective.

Observe the performer shown in figure 5.4. Notice how he moves to the rear from his ready position. As he steps backward, he maintains good eye contact with the ball and gets his body into a side-facing position prior to beginning the hit. Once he gets set for the hit (sequence G), he shifts the weight forward

Fig. 5.3 The Reverse Hop

(sequence *H*) and then begins strong shoulder rotation prior to the hit (sequences *I* and *J*). Note the good stable position during the hit. This is especially important when you go for a kill shot from deep in the back court.

In addition to the straight front wall and corner kill shots the skilled player also kills the balls on the fly and on the half volley. The *fly kill* is a very difficult shot to execute as great control and accuracy are required. You should not attempt this shot unless you are in good position and your opponent is either off balance or in the back court where it will be difficult for him to return the ball. The *half volley* or *pickup kill* is also very difficult to execute because it is very fast and requires maximum concentration. In both of these kill shots an underhand or sidearm stroke is used, and to be most effective hit the ball to a corner so that it strikes the side wall first. It must always be hit low. On the fly kill you should let the ball drop until it is about one foot off the floor before striking it. In the pickup your should strike the ball immediately as it rebounds from the floor.

When the ball is hit too hard or too high, it rebounds off the back wall and usually results in an easy kill shot for advanced player. Very few players use a straight shot to the front wall for a kill from a back wall recovery unless they have the shot perfected. Instead, it is better to hit at least one other wall before hitting the front wall in order to avoid a possible easy setup and to make following the ball more difficult. When the ball rebounds with great force off the back wall, you should respond by hitting the kill shot from a position close to the short line, thus making it easier for you to control and to place. A ceiling shot which rebounds from the back wall at least as high as your knees will also

Fig. 5.4   The Backup Rear Court Kill Shot

become an easy setup for a kill shot. It is executed as previously described for a kill shot, but requires much faster timing because of the sharper decline when the ball rebounds off the wall. Because of this angle, the swing is shorter whenever the ball is close to the back wall; indeed, at times the wrist snap is all that can be used.

Although it is not used frequently, an overhand stroke is sometimes used to execute a kill shot. In such situations the ball usually rebounds high from the floor; consequently this shot is used only when your opponent is in deep back court. The overhand kill can be hit on the fly or off a high bounce and should be directed to the corners.

The Ceiling Shot

When hitting a ceiling shot from the back court many good players use an underhand stroke in order to get a sharper angle and thus help prevent the ball from rebounding off the back wall. The ball should be hit with an open or slightly cupped hand to help guarantee greater control. It must be hit in the correct direction and with ample speed so that it strikes the ceiling close to the front wall, and the rebound off the front wall and floor will carry it to the back corner without any back or side wall play.

The Punch Ball Hit

In executing the ceiling shot, the passing shot, and at times the kill shot, you may use a *fist* or *punch ball hit*. An example of the ceiling shot is shown in figure 5.5. To execute this shot hold your fingers tightly curled across the palm of your hand so that the middle bones of the fingers are almost flush with the heel of the hand. Your thumb should be placed alongside the index finger and should not cross the knuckles as in the fist used in boxing. An underhand or sidearm stroke should be used in hitting the ball, and contact should be made at the junction of the knuckles and palm of your hand (sequence C). Great speed can be gained with this hit since the bony surface of the fingers does not allow the ball to be cushioned as it is when hit from the palm or at the base of the fingers. Because of the greater speed given the ball in this hit, the fist ball is used most often in a passing shot or when trying to get an opponent out of front court position. At times you may hit the ball directly at your opponent. The great speed will not permit him to get ready for the return and will prevent him from getting into position for a good return, especially if he is close to the front wall.

The fist ball can be used both offensively and defensively, but it is used predominantly as a defensive shot because control of the ball is difficult. This may be understood when you realize that the hitting area is much smaller and the more irregular surface of the fingers does not allow for the accuracy afforded by an open or cupped hand. This hit is effective when you must play your weak hand in order to gain additional speed and when control is not a major factor.

Fig. 5.5 The Underhand Ceiling Shot

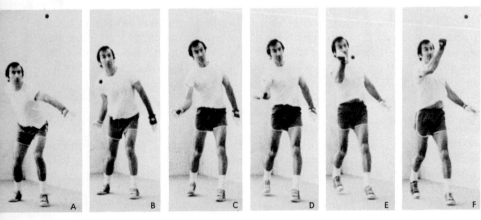

A   B   C   D   E   F

The Passing Shot

An effective passing shot is one that seems to hug the side wall. Tremendous control is required to hit the ball to the front wall so that it angles off parallel to the side wall. You should strike the ball with an open hand, wrist cocked but flexed at the last second to help impart some side spin so that the ball will come out at a straighter angle and remain close to the side wall. If your opponent anticipates this shot, you should be able to change your swing quickly and direct the ball to the opposite side. This shot is especially impressive when your opponent runs back expecting the ball to rebound off the side wall only to see it pass a few feet away from his position.

Once you are proficient in the shots just described, you may wish to try one or two trick shots. Although trick shots will not improve your game, they are useful in developing greater coordination and skill. These shots can also be used in exhibition because they are tremendous crowd pleasers. You should never use a trick shot during play as you will not have ample time to execute it effectively. All trick shots require careful planning and controlled execution. For example, see the straddle crotch shot demonstrated in figure 5.6. The ball is traveling slowly, allowing the player ample time to get into position for the hit. Notice his stable position and his concentration on the ball. If he fails to

Fig. 5.6   The Straddle Crotch Shot

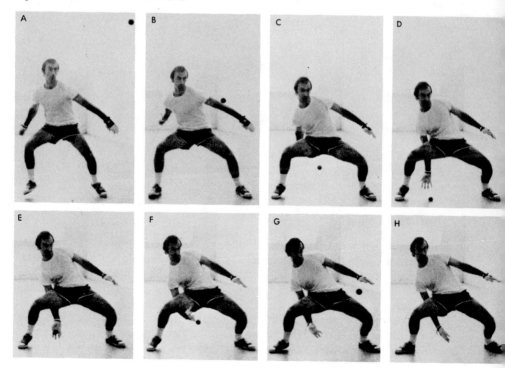

Fig. 5.7 The Sidearm Stroke Using the Nonpreferred Arm

remain steady or if he miscalculates the shot, what happens to him should not be difficult for you to figure out.

ADDITIONAL HINTS

As improvement continues, you should emphasize development of the weak arm until it can be used as effectively as the strong arm. You want to be able to do everything as well, if not better, with the weak arm as with the strong arm. Many top players through long, hard concentration on the weak arm actually develop stronger "weak" arms. A player executing a sidearm stroke with a well-developed nonpreferred arm is shown in figure 5.7. Compare this player's technique with that of the players shown in figure 3.16 and figure 3.21 who are executing the sidearm stroke with the preferred arm. There is practically no difference between how the sidearm stroke is executed with either the right or left hand among these players.

Use of both arms enables you to have better control of front-wall shots because of a greater variety of shots and strokes. By being in front court position, you force your opponents to hit to you, which also helps set up the kill shot.

When playing a fast, hard game, you should not overstretch to get off a shot, but try instead to take an extra step in order to get into a position where you can put more power and control into the shot. Many tall players have a tendency to overstretch because of their long reach, but they should avoid this action. Although a fast ball is an asset in a hard, fast-moving game you should also be aware that speed without control is of little value.

There are other shots and skills that you can employ, but many are individual preference rather than basic elements. For example, when playing a high rebound off the back wall, you could stay close to the back wall and hit a ceiling shot with the overhand stroke. Also, you can learn to turn what appears to be a certain shot into a completely different one. For example, when you are ready to hit a ceiling shot and see your opponent move to the rear court in anticipation of the return, you should come down on the ball with the overhand stroke and execute a kill shot. Use of this and other shots depends upon your strategy at a given time and upon the shot you can perform successfully under existing circumstances.

Game strategy

6

STRATEGY FOR SINGLES PLAY

One of the best ways to begin developing your pattern of play is to think in terms of court position and whether you are on the offense or defense. You should always try to hold a position in the center of the court or on an imaginary line running through the center of the floor from front to back. This is the most advantageous position, for you can play to either side by taking a step or two or you can move up or back as the situation demands.

If this position is maintained, your chances of being caught out of position will be very slim. Your opponent will be taxed in trying to get the ball away from you. Be ready to move in any direction. After hitting a shot move back into position immediately. Do not wait to see where your shot went or relax because it looked like a sure point. Once back into position you will again be in the most advantageous area for a return and usually will have time to think in terms of the next shot or of how to retrieve the ball most effectively. If you are not in the correct position, your opponent will be able to hit the ball away from you; you will find yourself constantly running after the ball with little chance of returning it.

Being on the center line in front court is also very important since you do not look back to see where your opponent is hitting the ball. Keeping your eyes focused on the front wall, you try to pick up the ball with peripheral vision and make the necessary move accordingly. You should also learn to listen for sounds in order to anticipate where your opponent is and to listen for the exact moment of the hit in order to prepare for the ball. By utilizing your senses, you can often determine in advance what return to expect and from where to expect it.

The position you take on the court depends greatly on the shots that your opponent uses. If your opponent, for example, always tries to kill the ball, you should position yourself a little closer to the front wall, just inside the short line. If he constantly tries to pass you, you should stand a little deeper in the court, one or two feet behind the short line. You will then be in a better receiving position and be able to make more returns with greater effectiveness. You should try to get in front of your opponent in the front and front center court position; by doing this, you are in a better position to return crucial kill shots and to execute the kill and passing shots. In essence, you can control the front wall, a very important factor in scoring.

You should work to develop both a strong offense and a strong defense. When on the offensive, try to go for the kill or for a put-away, and when on the defensive, try to keep the ball in play until your opponent commits an error or until you can regain the offensive position. Most court play consists of a struggle to gain the center court position, which is considered the offensive position. The main objective is to secure and maintain this position with offensive shots, forcing your opponent to be on the move constantly while you direct the play. In order to retain this position it is necessary to keep your opponent in the back court or at least behind you; to accomplish this, use deep shots such as passing and ceiling shots. A rally usually does not last long; so you should try for a put-away as soon as the opportunity arises. This is most easily accomplished by getting your opponent out of position and then placing the next shot so that he will be unable to reach it or to play it well.

The server has the advantage in attaining center court position. This is why it is so important to have a good serve. If you serve weakly, your opponent can very easily put you on the defensive with a strong return. The main objective of the service therefore should be to score an ace or at least to force your opponent into a weak return. To be in the best position for the service return, you should get in the center of the court approximately one to two feet behind the short line. Without an effective serve or by not attaining proper position, the server quickly loses the offense and is put on the defense.

The possibility of scoring an ace or forcing your opponent to hit a weak return depends to a great extent upon your opponent's weaknesses. You therefore should analyze your opponent's strokes and shots when you are warming up with him before starting the game. You should determine at which height, with what speed, and in which direction you should hit the ball in order to secure the most effective results. If you notice that your opponent has trouble with his left arm, you should serve to the left side; if he has trouble with his overhead strokes, you should hit high shots to the corners; and if he has trouble handling hard hit balls, you should use power shots. Analyzation should not stop after the game begins, but should continue so that you can constantly readjust your shots in terms of weaknesses discovered. This is a fundamental rule in handball: always play to your opponent's weak points and never play to his strong points, except occasionally to keep him from expecting the ball on the same side at all times.

If you are on the defense and wish to go on the offense, you must drive your opponent out of center court position into the back court. To do this you use a passing shot, a lob, or a ceiling shot. Be careful not to hit the ball at such

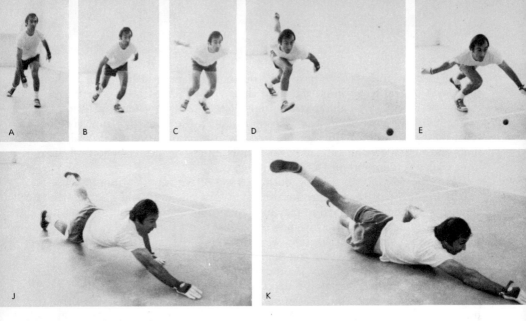

Fig. 6.1 The Dive Shot

an angle that it will rebound straight off the back wall, for this can result in an easy kill or pass setup. Because you are the receiver of the service, your most advantageous position is approximately five to six feet from the back wall. From this position you can move in any direction to return the ball and force the server to move out of his controlling position. You should think of the return of service as one of the most important shots of the game.

The importance of using a variety of serves can be demonstrated. If the server consistently hits to one side, the receiver should stand more to that side, neutralizing the effectiveness of the serve by shortening the amount of time necessary to get to the ball and by being prepared for the serve before it is hit. Such anticipation is not possible unless your opponent consistently uses the same serve. A good player does not fall into the habit of hitting the same shots or serves over and over. Your opponent soon capitalizes on your habitual actions. It is important to have a large repertoire of shots and not to rely solely on a few strong shots.

When you play offensively, it is important to keep your opponent off stride so that he cannot get set for an effective return which would drive you out of center court position. You can achieve this if you play every shot with a definite plan, placing it in a particular spot. Aimless return of the ball keeps you in trouble and does not contribute to the development of skill or strategy. Use different shots, change pace, and make different placements. In this way you will keep your opponent off balance and make him play to your advantage. For example, a soft, easy shot after a rally of hard-hit, fast-moving balls is usually sufficient to throw your timing off even if you are a top-level player. In placing the ball you should try the following effective hits: low at your opponent's feet; hard and fast directly at him when he is very close to the front wall;

close to the side wall so that he hesitates to take a full swing; rebounds off one or two side walls to prevent the ball from coming straight out and to put spin on the ball.

The important factors in keeping the offensive are to be aggressive and to have confidence in your ability. If you begin to fret over certain shots or become flustered when you are being beaten, your chances of losing the game are greatly increased. You have undoubtedly seen or heard of an athlete who beat himself, usually because of his inability to cope with unexpected situations —a bad play on his part, a spectacular play by his opponent, and so forth. Under such circumstances this player may begin to press his shots only to find that instead of improving, his game becomes progressively worse. In such situations, force yourself to relax and take more time on your shots and placements. You will then begin to hit the ball effectively, which in turn will help you to regain your confidence.

Aggressiveness is a quality that must be developed, for not only will it cause your opponent to press his game, but it can also be the deciding factor in your game. To be aggressive you should try for every shot. There is not a shot, except for a kill rollout, that cannot be returned if you can reach it. Positioning therefore is very important. If you are trying to return a well-executed shot, you may have to resort to still other measures to get to the ball, including diving after a kill or fairly low hit shot (fig. 6.1), leaping for a high ball, and climbing a wall to avoid banging into it on a sharp break to the side. In all cases try for every shot; do not let any shots go uncontested, even when you think there is no chance for a return. You will probably amaze yourself when you see how many balls you return by doing this. Your confidence will be increased and your opponent's shattered.

When you are losing, it is usually a good idea to change your style of play. For example, if you have been trying for a kill on every shot, go for more passing or ceiling shots. If you have been using a power-type game, go for more control and easy placements, with lobs and ceiling shots. If you find that you are having difficulty with a certain shot, do not try it for a few points and pick it up later. If you are playing a winning game, maintain the same style. If your margin is sufficiently great however, it is a good idea to experiment with different innovations, but keep the same basic game.

One of the main objectives of four-wall handball is to keep your opponent on the run and to force him to take difficult shots. This is true at all levels of skill, but becomes decreasingly important as your skill improves. For the very advanced player there are few very hard shots, and it is almost impossible to keep your opponent constantly on the run. The level of skill is so high that execution of one shot can completely change the picture of play, and the game becomes a battle of minds rather than of strength and speed.

To play on this level takes maturation which is at least partially the result of practice and play at all levels of competition. You should begin to develop the ability to anticipate, to think ahead, to make quick decisions, and to analyze your game and your opponent's game. The more thoughtful game you play the more improvement you will see in your tactics and all around ability to play. You will also win many more games and develop greater confidence in yourself.

Many cases can be cited of examples of anticipation, thinking ahead, last minute decision making, and player analyzation. An obvious example is when you feint your opponent into hitting the ball where you want it by making a definite move in one direction but then immediately reversing as your opponent makes his hit. The hitter in this situation will be trying to hit away from you and will hit in the opposite direction of your feint. If you want to fake your opponent out of position, you should set yourself as in making a definite shot. Then as your opponent anticipates the shot and moves to position himself for it, you should hit the ball at a different angle at the last possible moment. When your opponent is caught out of position on one side of the court, he will expect the ball down the opposite side, and as he makes his move, hit the ball to the side where he was originally positioned. Whenever your opponent is set in good position for an expected kill shot, you should hit an easy high shot or ceiling shot to the back court.

In executing the kill shot do not try to roll it out, but take into consideration your opponent's position in the court, his physical condition, and the score of the game. If the score is well in your favor and your opponent is very fast, you should go for a low, flat kill to avoid any possible return. When your opponent is caught in deep back court and is not very fast, you should hit a relatively high, safe kill or a soft kill to avoid any chance of error.

If you are alert and in good position, many other equally effective plays can be made merely by catching mistakes made by your opponent. For example, if on an attempted ceiling shot the ball does not hit the ceiling but hits the front wall first, a fly-kill setup or an easy back wall setup may arise. If a ceiling shot is angled too sharply, the ball may hit the side wall on the rebound off the floor and become an easy setup for a kill or passing shot. It is only by observing your opponent and his shots that you can take advantage of his mistakes and anticipate a shot in time for proper positioning. There are many possibilities that arise and each must be resolved at the moment it happens if the end result is to be in your favor. Thus it is important to think of what you will do when a specific situation presents itself before it occurs. This is usually done whenever there is a lull in the game, between a rally, or during a time-out. Do not be hesitant to talk to yourself during the game as it will help keep you relaxed and attuned to what should be done in specific situations.

STRATEGY FOR DOUBLES PLAY

Most of the preceding descriptions of play and the various strategies used are also applicable to the game of doubles. Because of the addition of two more players, the court is usually much better covered and requires greater accuracy in placements. Even more important is the teamwork developed by each team, for you must share responsibilities in covering the court and in determining who is to take various hits when both players have an opportunity to return the ball.

The best doubles teams are not always composed of the best singles players, but more often are developed when each partner complements the other in terms of the strong hand, physical abilities, strongest shots, type of play, and other factors. If the strong points of one partner make up for the weak points of the other, the combination usually is quite effective and successful. Two top singles players usually have a tendency to play a singles game and take many shots which should be played by the other partner. It is possible to develop a strong doubles team by constantly practicing together so that each partner knows instinctively which ball he should play and can anticipate his partner's actions. Before beginning play each team should decide, through analyzation of their strong and weak points, which side of the court each player will play. The player with the stronger left arm should play the left side in order to cover that side most effectively and the player with the stronger right arm, the right side.

To define court responsibilities you should divide the court in such a manner that a definite playing arrangement can be exercised. The main objective of any arrangement is to play side by side in front court position so that no balls can get by. Remember that when you are up front you are on offense, and if you drop back to the rear court, you are on defense. So important is this front position that you should try to take every ball that comes your way and to return it as effectively as possible in order to keep your front court position and to keep your opponents in the back court. If this position can be maintained, it will not be long before you get a chance for a kill shot which will end the rally. In this position the left-side player should take most balls in the middle court because of his stronger right arm. All balls hit to the back court or balls hit at a sharp angle of rebound off the front and side walls should be taken by the player on the side toward which the ball is travelling.

If both players take all the shots hit on the side on which they are positioned, they soon find themselves out of position and vulnerable for a put-away. If the left-side player, for example, tries to return all balls coming out of the left-hand corner, he has to run into the right side of the court, thus leaving the left side unguarded. The same applies to the right-side player who tries to return all balls coming out of the right corner. In addition, he must use his weak left arm for many shots. Sharply hit angle shots off the front wall should be allowed to rebound off the side wall if hit sufficiently high and taken by the player on the opposite side (fig. 6.2).

When players play side by side, it is imperative that each player cover for his partner whenever he is caught out of position. Thus, if your partner is caught in the back court, be prepared for a quick return volley to the front court on his side. If it is anticipated in time, you can then hit a slow lob or corner ceiling shot to drive your opponent back and give your partner ample time to get back into position. Since it is not always possible to cover well in such situations, it is imperative for the player in the back court to immediately come up to his front court position after returning the ball. The best position in doubles is for each partner to stand just back of the short line equidistant from the other and from the side wall. This is a little closer than in singles, but is necessary in order to return all low hit balls to the front court and at the same time through alert coverage by each partner to cover the back court. Because of this close front court position, a hard, fast drive at your opponent's feet can prove very effective as there is less time for him to maneuver into the proper position. A well-placed shot can also be used for passing purposes whenever it is very hard.

Rallies in a game of doubles usually last longer than in singles because of better court coverage which makes it difficult to hit a shot that cannot be returned. Most shots are defensive, whether they be hit up front or in the back court, until an opportunity occurs to use an offensive shot. This makes it necessary for you always to think ahead one or two shots, working to get your opponent out of position or to make a mistake so that you can come in with a kill.

Since these offensive opportunities occur less frequently in doubles, you should always be on the alert to observe and capitalize on them. To help elicit these mistakes or to outmaneuver your opponents, you must, as in singles, analyze both of your opponents' possible weaknesses. When you have determined who has less ability or is weak in certain shots, relay this information to your partner, and then both of you should concentrate your attack on these weaknesses.

Many top doubles teams (both right-handed) prefer an arrangement in which the right-side player covers the front court and that area included to the right of an imaginary line drawn from the left-hand corner to the rear right-hand corner (fig. 6.3). If the ball is high when coming out of the left-hand corner, the right-side player should let it rebound off the right side wall so that his partner can take it from the better position with his right hand. The left-side player should take all balls hit a few feet high out of the right-hand corner so that the strong arm can once again be used. Such cross-balance coverage makes it difficult to hit kill shots in the front court. The right-side player must, however, be very skilled in the kill shot, while the left-side player must be highly skilled in back wall play and ability to cover the court, for usually most shots are directed to him.

If a team is composed of a right-handed player and a left-handed player, the left-handed player should play the left side and the right-handed, the right side. Such a combination is very strong on the side wall shots because of the strong arm on each side. If playing against such a team you should direct many

Front Wall

Front Wall

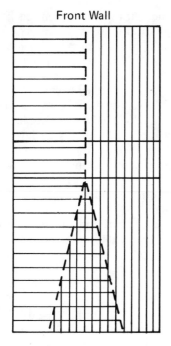

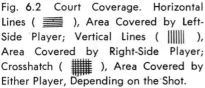

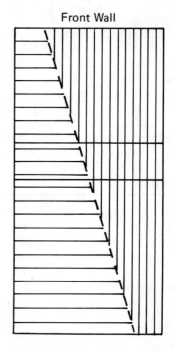

Fig. 6.2 Court Coverage. Horizontal Lines (▤), Area Covered by Left-Side Player; Vertical Lines (‖‖‖), Area Covered by Right-Side Player; Crosshatch (▦), Area Covered by Either Player, Depending on the Shot.

Fig. 6.3 Court Coverage. Horizontal Lines (▤), Area Covered by Left-Side Player; Vertical Lines (‖‖‖), Area Covered by Right-Side Player.

returns down the middle between the players so that they have to use their weak arm. It usually is rare, however, for a player not to return a ball hit down the middle.

Most of the serves used in singles play are not equally effective in doubles because the receivers are much closer to the corners. Receivers should be positioned as in singles, but with each partner side by side, equidistant from each other and the side walls. The most effective serves therefore are those that are sharply angled, that bounce at the receiver's feet, and that go into the corners for an unpredictable angle of rebound. To increase the effectiveness of your serves you should fake the direction of your serves, use different speeds for your serves, and vary the kinds of serves. You should also serve from the center or on your side of the center of the service zone in order to be in proper position for the return. At times the position of the receivers will help you in determining which serve to use. For example, if the receivers stand close to the short line and continually try to volley the serve, you should hit the ball hard and low off the side wall. You may also elect to hit a corner shot to drive them back, but the shot must be sufficiently high so that they cannot volley it. An occasional crosscourt serve is also effective as in an easy high shot very close to the side wall where your opponents will not be able to return the ball with any degree of accuracy or power.

Each player should play every shot and at the same time be ready to remain in or attain good defensive position as soon as he sees that his partner is taking the shot. This cover of your partner will pay many dividends: for example, when your partner decides at the last moment to let the ball go by in your favor or if by chance he misses the shot. When one player receives the serve, the other should quickly move up to the front court for defense, as should the receiver after hitting the ball.

Players should always talk to each other during and after a hand-out or point. During play, the talk should consist mainly of indicating the taking of shots by calling "mine" or "yours." Talk should be short and concise. It is also good practice to give words of praise such as "good shot" or "good cover" because this helps keep up morale and confidence. Words of encouragement should also be given when needed—when the ball is dead or not in play so that you do not hold up the game. A team is very hard to beat if each player knows that his partner has faith and confidence in him.

It should be mentioned here that some players think it is good strategy to "stretch" the rules. This occurs when on an easy back wall setup your opponent purposely positions himself in a direct line with your shot so that it will hit him for a hinder which calls for a replay. Players should avoid this practice at all times because, aside from being illegal, it defeats the basic premise of the game: each player should have an unobstructed view and shot at the ball and there should be no interference with the shot.

Rules of the game and court etiquette

7

The discussion in this chapter does not include an explanation of the rules of the game since a copy of official rules can easily be obtained from most sporting goods stores and wherever handball is played. However, certain basic knowledge and explanation are necessary for playing a high-level game. Other than in a championship match, referees are seldom present during play; consequently responsibility for legal play rests with the players. In informal or pick-up games the participants are not only players, but also referees and scorekeepers. It is important, therefore, for you to have a good understanding of the rules so that you can recognize infractions and enact the appropriate penalties. Also, to help make the game go smoothly you should know and practice various court courtesies.

PLAYING REGULATIONS

To decide who serves first in a regulation match a coin is tossed. When no referee is present, various other methods can be employed such as a rebound toss to the short line or back wall. You must start and complete the serve from anywhere in the service zone, which is bounded by the short line and the service line (a line running parallel to the short line five feet closer to the front wall). Stepping on lines is permissable, but stepping over a line in the act of serving is a *fault*. Two such faults constitute an *out* (hand-out or side-out). To serve drop the ball on the floor and then strike it on its first bounce from the floor. If you attempt to hit the ball and fail to do so, you are out, and you are also out if you bounce the ball more than three times in the service zone before serving—before contacting the ball. Before serving the ball, you should be sure that your opponent is ready. If you quick serve, the point is replayed without penalty. You may request time-out after a point or hand-out in order to wipe your glasses or face and to take care of other necessary detail. The time-out must not exceed 30 seconds, however, and not more than three time-outs are granted to each player or side in a game.

In a legal serve, the ball must pass the short line before it can be returned. This prevents the receiver from charging the ball as soon as it is hit by the server. If your served ball fails to bounce on the floor behind the short line, the serve is termed a *short* and must be replayed. Two consecutive shorts constitute an out, and your opponent then becomes the server. Also illegal are those serves which hit the ceiling, back wall, or two side walls before hitting the floor behind the short line. An illegally served ball may not be played and must be re-served unless it is the second such short serve, and then it is an out.

On the service and during play, the ball should be dry. Any violation of this rule results in forfeiture of the serve. A wet ball permits the server to put additional spin on the ball, which gives him an unfair advantage similar to that of a baseball pitcher who pitches a spitball. In a match the referee may put a new ball in play if the ball is wet or require a player to change gloves if they are too wet.

In doubles, the server's partner must stand within the service box with his back to the wall and with both feet on the floor until the ball passes the short line. In this way he does not interfere with the receiver's vision or gain unfair advantage by getting into position early. If your partner is hit by a served fly ball while standing in the service box, this counts as a *dead ball* without penalty, but does not eliminate any short or fault preceding this serve. If your partner is hit by the served ball on the bounce, the serve is a short ball. If he moves out of the service box in order to avoid being hit by the served ball, the move constitutes a violation. If he is hit during such movement, he is penalized by an out, and the ball is automatically dead. When the served ball passes behind your partner and strikes the floor behind the short line, it is a dead ball, but does not eliminate a short preceding this serve. Many times the ball may pass behind your partner when he flexes his knees, head or trunk in order to avoid being hit, but if his feet are on the ground and his back is to the side wall, no penalty is incurred.

As a receiver you must stand at least five feet back of the short line while the ball is being served. You are required to play a legal serve either on the fly or on the first bounce. Whenever there is an illegal service, play immediately stops, and any play of the ball that follows is void. To eliminate any misunderstanding you should not catch or stop, in any way, an illegally served ball, even if it appears obvious.

During play if the ball is swung at and missed, you or your partner may continue your attempt to play the ball again before the second bounce. This occurs occasionally when you miss an attempt on a hard-hit ball in midcourt but can still play the ball upon its rebound off the back wall. Many times your opponent may be behind you in such situations, and if he is hit by the ball after you miss in your attempt, the hit counts against him—either a point or handout as the case may be.

Unintentional interference by your opponent in your attempt to run to the back wall for the second try is termed a *hinder*, and the point must be replayed. A hinder also occurs when a returned ball hits your opponent before striking the floor, even if the ball continues to the front wall or travels toward the back wall. In this case, as in all legal unintentional hinders, the ball is dead, and the point must be replayed. Another frequent hinder occurs when you unintentionally interfere with your opponent, thus preventing him from having a fair chance to return the ball. To avoid causing such hinders you should always move toward the front wall out of the way of the oncoming ball. Your movement should always be toward the center of the court so that you do not get caught with your back up against the side wall only to watch the ball go by when you are out of position. In a regulation match the referee is empowered to call a hinder, but when no referee is present, the call becomes your responsibility.

Decisions regarding hinders should be liberal to discourage the practice of playing the ball where your adversary cannot see it until too late to prepare for the hit. To say that the ball was killed or that your opponent could not get to it is not acceptable, for each player is entitled to a fair chance to recover the ball. This rule is abused by players who consider it a weak reason for having the play repeated. They feel that as long as a player can get his hand on the ball it should be played and only when physical contact with an opponent is made, preventing him from reaching the ball or executing a swing, should a hinder be called. This practice is in opposition to the main intent of the game and should be avoided as much as possible. In doubles, interference from your partner it is not a hinder. Hinders can occur only between opponents.

A ball passing between your legs, a straddled ball, is sometimes considered a hinder. The decision depends upon whether the ball was obscured from sight or the action interfered with following the flight of the ball. This occurs when you jump up or split your legs to avoid getting hit by the ball, especially when you are close to the front wall. In the case of a screen ball, when the legally served ball returns from the front wall so close to the server that he obstructs your view of the ball, the ball is immediately dead, and the point should be replayed. It does not void any previous short ball.

Remember that it is the duty of the side that has played the ball to get out of the way of the opponents. You cannot just hold your position after the hit or move in any direction, even to gain center court position, so that view of the ball or the play by your opponent is obstructed. In such cases an avoidable hinder occurs; this is also known as the hinder point or out, depending upon whether the offender was receiving or serving. Avoidable hinders occur when you move into a position to effect a block, when you do not move sufficiently to allow your opponent his shot, and when you move in the way of, and are struck by, the ball just played by your opponent. For example, let us assume that your opponent hits a weak shot that comes straight off the back wall for what seems to be an easy return for a kill or passing shot. He then moves a few feet behind the short line and places himself directly in the line of your hit so that when you hit the ball it strikes him in the back.

Care should be exercised in calling an avoidable hinder because many times what looks like an avoidable hinder is purely unintentional action. The deciding factor should be whether your opponent made some attempt to get out of your way even though it was relatively impossible to do so. A court hinder occurs when the ball hits an obstruction in the playing court such as a door latch or a protruding window, light, or air duct and rebounds in an abnormal manner. There is no penalty on such a hinder, and the play involving that point must be done over.

The foregoing discussion, shows that the rules governing handball are straightforward and do not require lengthy explanation and/or interpretation. This is one of the reasons why handball is so enjoyable. It is simple to play, but is also a top-level game requiring the highest degree of skill.

COURT ETIQUETTE

To enjoy the game of handball to the utmost, you must abide by certain unwritten rules and traditions. Because of the close quarters and the intimacy of play, all players must exemplify the highest ideals of sportsmanship in order to enjoy a smooth and uncontested game.

As in most other sports, you should introduce yourself to your opponent at the beginning of play if you do not know him and let him know your caliber of play. If you are a beginner and he is a class A player, it would not be fair to him to play with you because you would not be able to give him a good game. In such a case he then finds another player more equal in ability, and you do likewise. Unless there are extenuating circumstances, however, most players do not refuse to play either with or against a poorer player as long as the difference is within reasonable limits. For most effective and worthwhile play both players should be of about the same ability. It takes very little time to discover the truth about a "verbal game" once play begins.

As handball requires much deep concentration and anticipation it is important that there be no unnecessary talk during a rally or between plays. There is nothing more infuriating to a player to have his thinking disrupted by constant chattering. This does not mean that you should be completely silent throughout a game, for many times a few words are called for or needed. It is proper, for example, to compliment your opponent when he makes a very good shot or *dig*, the return of a ball that appeared to be impossible to return. Politeness indicates that you recognize skilled play; complimenting your opponent shows your respect and admiration. Recognition of your opponent's good play shows good sportsmanship. Spectators should behave in the same manner.

Whenever a serious question arises during play, you should give your honest opinion regarding the point in question. If it is not possible to come to a conclusion, you should agree to play the point over. Many times your opponent may be in a position where he cannot see your hit or the outcome of your shot.

It is therefore necessary for you to call the play as soon as it happens. This occurs often on a dig where it is difficult to ascertain whether the return was made off the first or second bounce. Sometimes it is hard to determine if a kill shot hit the floor before it hit the front wall. If your opponent expresses or shows doubt regarding the legitimacy of the play, the point should be replayed. If your opponent calls the shot and is in the most advantageous position to do so, you should accept his decision without question.

During play, you should call all your illegal hits: for example, when you hit the ball on your wrist or arm or when you make a double hit. Often such hits can be recognized when the ball takes off in an unexpected direction or can be determined by the sound produced by the hit. If the game has been in progress for any length of time, an illegal hit on the arm or wrist will result in a wet ball because of the perspiration. Discovery of a wet ball after a supposedly good hit is quite disconcerting and leads to disrespect.

Before serving, you should always examine the ball to see if it is wet. If it is, dry it; wipe the ball with a dry portion of your clothing or with a towel or by rolling the ball on the floor under your foot. Before putting the ball into play, you should then let your opponent examine it so that it meets with his satisfaction. This practice is very important when playing conditions are very hot or humid. You should wear a light cotton shirt to absorb perspiration and to help prevent accidents which may occur if perspiration gets on the floor.

One of the most exacting phases of play requiring high-level sportsmanship is the calling of hinders. You may have a tendency to play it safe and not call a hinder so that your opponent will not think you are taking advantage by canceling what appears to have been a good shot. A general rule of thumb for such cases is this: if your opponent legitimately interfered with your shot, either by being too close to you or by obstructing your view of the ball, call a hinder. More important, you should always attempt, honestly, not to interfere with the person trying for a return. You should move out of his way so that he can follow the ball and be able to execute his stroke. even if it sometimes means giving up a strategic position. Only in this way can fewer hinders be called and a faster, and cleaner game be enjoyed. This is especially true in doubles, for in this case the chances for hinders are twice as many.

Call a hinder only when you are involved in the play. You should not be in the back court and call a hinder when your opponent makes a kill from front court position, for you could not follow the play all the way and would have no possible chance of returning the ball. Nor should it be necessary for you to make body contact with your opponent to prove that you cannot execute a shot or reach the ball. You should respect your opponent's decisions, and when serious doubt arises, there should be a discussion of the rules in order to clarify any misunderstanding. Most handball players display admirable integrity in abiding by the rules, and thus they can play excellent games without the services of a referee. Good players do not look for ways to circumvent the rules so that they can gain a point or two.

During certain hours of the day when handball courts are in full use, the

---

If you and your opponent cannot decide whether a shot was legitimate, what should be done? Whose responsibility is it to call illegal hits?

---

length of time allotted players must sometimes be limited. In such cases it is customary to let the team playing finish its game even if by so doing you shorten your own reserved playing time. When the next team arrives, you should limit your game by reducing the number of points needed to decide the winner. In this way you can complete your game and not take more than a few minutes of the next team's time.

When playing a friendly, courteous game, you should alternate your serves to either side when playing singles and to alternate receivers when playing doubles. This method ensures equal opportunity to play strong and weak shots. Also, in keeping score the server should call out the score at the end of each rally and/or prior to each serve.

Play hard but play fairly. If you want to be respected, never resort to unfair tactics.

Appendix: Questions and answers

MULTIPLE CHOICE

1. Specific warm-up prior to actual game play is most useful in:
   A. specific coordinations as when executing certain shots
   b. allowing you to start play on a higher physical level
   c. increasing your heart rate to allow you to perform on a higher level
   d. generalized stretching for greater flexibility   (p. 52)

2. The spread in popularity of handball in the United States is generally attributed to:
   a. the colleges and universities
   B. athletic clubs
   c. the YMCA
   d. a group of top players who gave demonstrations before large crowds in the big cities   (p. 3)

3. When you are winning and have a comfortable point margin it is a good idea:
   a. to change your style in order to experiment with new approaches
   b. to ease up in your play to help conserve energy for later play in case you have to play three games
   C. to maintain the same style of play and experiment with different innovations
   d. to let your opponent get a few more points so that you may have a closer game   (p. 71)

4. The fly hit can be executed:
   A. with the ball at the height which calls for a kill, passing or ceiling shot
   b. most effectively with the overhand stroke
   c. only when you have ample time to prepare for the hit
   d. only when you are in front court position   (p. 36)

5. Before a skill is truly learned:
   a. you must practice it until you can repeat it at least once out of every four or five tries
   B. there must be a strong nervous pathway from the brain to the muscles involved
   c. there must be much mental but little physical practice of the skill

d. you must undergo much physical strain as by exhausting yourself during practice periods   (p. 15)

6. A served ball which hits the rear wall before bouncing on the floor beyond the short line is:
   a. illegal and is served over without penalty
   b. called a long
   C. called a short
   d. a fault and the server loses the serve   (p. 78)

7. The main objective of the kill shot is to:
   a. force your opponent out of position
   b. get a roll out so that the ball cannot be returned
   c. force your opponent to "work" in his returns to help fatigue him
   D. create a rebound so low that it is virtually impossible to return   (p. 28)

8. The most effective kill shot is one in which the ball first hits:
   a. the front wall and then the side wall in the corner
   B. the side wall and then the front wall in the corner
   c. the front wall and then rebounds straight out
   d. the front wall and then the side wall approximately four to five feet from the front wall   (p. 28)

9. In the passing shot the ball should:
   a. rebound off the rear wall close to the side wall
   b. rebound off the side wall in the area of the short line
   C. not strike the floor or side wall until it has passed your opponent
   d. strike the floor close to the side wall in the service area   (p. 32)

10. The most important stroke (in terms of use and effectiveness) is the:
   a. overhand stroke   c. overhand-sidearm stroke
   b. underhand stroke   D. sidearm stroke   (p. 17)

11. To most effectively execute the power serve you should position yourself:
   A. as close to the right side wall as possible
   b. as close to the left side wall as possible
   c. approximately in the middle of the service area
   d. anywhere in the service area where you feel most comfortable   (p. 20)

12. In the diagonal serve the ball, after rebounding off the second side wall, should:
   a. drop sharply toward the floor and rear wall
   B. "come out" straight, almost parallel to the rear wall
   c. "jump" up into the rear wall
   d. rebound off the rear wall and come out close to the side wall   (p. 23)

13. In the swing (downswing) initial forward body movement begins with the:
   a. hand followed by the arm, shoulders, trunk, hips, and legs
   B. legs followed by the hips, trunk, shoulders, and arm
   c. hips followed by the trunk, shoulders, arm and hand
   d. shoulders and arm followed by the trunk, hips, and legs   (pp. 12, 13)

14. In the ready position, you should assume a position in which you:
   a. are in a deep crouch   C. can move easily in any direction
   b. are able to move forward quickly   d. keep the arms bent and up high
                                                    (p. 8)

15. In the ready position you should:
   A. have your weight borne in the middle of your feet

b. have your weight on the balls of your feet
c. be facing the side wall
d. have your weight borne on the heels of your feet   (p. 9)

16. In doubles the main objective of any team arrangement should be to:
    a. play up and back to be able to receive all short and long hit balls
    b. play one man in the left front corner and one in the back right corner,
        to force your opponent to hit where you can go for the put-a-way
    C. play side by side so that no balls can get by when in front court position
    d. play one man in the right front corner and one in the left rear corner to
        stop most kill shots by your opponents   (p. 47)

17. The "workhouse" shot in handball is usually considered to be the:
    A. passing shot   c. kill shot
    b. the lob shot   d. ceiling shot   (p. 32)

18. For the majority of hits the ball should be contacted:
    a. in the palm of the hand
    b. with the finger tips
    c. with a tight fist
    D. at the base of the fingers and junction of the palm   (p. 8)

19. During a rally your opponent who is standing behind you is hit by the ball
    which glanced off your hand in an attempt to return the ball to the front wall.
    a. you therefore lose the point (or serve)
    B. a hinder is called
    c. you win the point (or serve)
    d. you call a block and win the point (or serve)   (p. 79)

20. While positioned behind your opponent who swings at the ball and misses it,
    you catch the ball before the second bounce.
    a. you therefore win the point (or serve)
    B. you lose the point (or serve)
    c. a hinder is called
    d. interference is called and the point is played over   (p. 78)

21. To drive your opponent out of front court position you should try for a:
    a. kill shot   c. side wall—front-wall hit
    b. rear wall hit   D. ceiling shot   (p. 35)

22. One of the most important factors which will force your opponent to press
    his game is:
    a. the execution of well-placed shots
    B. aggressiveness
    c. anticipating where he will hit the ball
    d. trying to appear as though you are not trying for many shots, but still re-
        turning most of his hits   (p. 71)

23. To gain greater accuracy in your hits you should:
    a. look at the spot where you want to hit the ball
    B. look at the ball during the hit
    c. look at your hand during the backswing and downswing
    d. look to one side and direct the hit to the other side   (pp. 38, 56)

24. To best develop quality you should do:
    a. long distance running
    b. short sprints at maximum speed

    c. stop and go running at maximum speed

    D. side, front and rear cutting movements   (p. 49)

25. In doubles, to hit a fast hard rebound off the front wall when positioned close to the front wall you should:

    a. keep your hand in cupped position

    b. immediately turn to face the side wall

    C. hit the ball with a relatively straight arm and hand when facing the front wall

    d. allow the ball to rebound off the rear wall   (p. 37)

26. The most effective, in terms of power and line of flight, passing shot is hit:

    a. with an underhand stroke

    b. with a straight arm overhand stroke

    C. with a bent arm overhand stroke

    d. with a fist or punch ball hit   (p. 32)

TRUE OR FALSE

t F 27. The most important phases of the swing are the backswing and follow-through. (p. 15)

t F 28. For maximum power in the hit you should take a modified backswing so that more power can be applied to the hit. (p. 15)

t F 29. Initial contact with the ball occurs when the ball is in front of the forward leg. (p. 13)

t F 30. Good footwork is characteristic of a top player but it is not essential to a beginner for proper execution of most shots (pp. 10, 57)

t F 31. The most advantageous position for hitting the ball is when you are facing the front wall during the hit. (p. 10)

t F 32. In preparation for the side-arm hit you shift your weight to the rear by leaning your trunk and shoulders to the rear. (p. 17)

T f 33. To help insure that the force and momentum produced in the swing is not decreased, it is necessary to follow-through in the hit. (p. 14)

T f 34. In the underhand stroke the arm stays relatively close to the body in the vertical plane as it passes the front of the body during the swing. (p. 16)

t F 35. In the power serve the ball should rebound off the rear wall close to the side wall. (p. 20)

T f 36. In the lob serve the ball should just reach the rear wall after rebounding off the floor. (p. 23)

T f 37. As a general rule a good player will hit a two-wall kill shot rather than a one-wall kill shot. (p. 28)

t F 38. The lob shot is used most often as an offensive shot. (p. 35)

t F 39. When serving it is good strategy to vary the speed of the serve but not the type of serve, especially if you have a strong serve. (p. 27)

T f 40. Decisions regarding which shot or stroke is to be used, should be made when the ball first comes off the front wall and often well before. (p. 57)

t F 41. Generally speaking, the soft kill is as effective as the regular kill and so it is used as often during play. (p. 30)

T f 42. In back wall play you should turn your body in the same direction that that the ball is traveling, especially when the ball is coming out of the rear corner. (p. 30)

T f 43. In back wall play you should usually let the ball drop to a very low height before contacting it in execution of your hit. (p. 30)

t F 44. The term "pick the ball off" usually refers to hitting the ball immediately as it rebounds off the floor. (p. 37)

t F 45. For most effective execution of the various shots it is not necessary to be standing parallel to the line of flight of the ball. (p. 28)

T f 46. In order to make quick and accurate decisions it is necessary to be in good physical condition for playing handball. (p. 41)

t F 47. To develop speed and accuracy in your hit you should begin by hitting easy until you can control the ball. (p. 14)

t F 48. When hitting the ball during competitive play, it is not necessary to direct it to a predetermined spot on the front wall. (p. 56)

T f 49. The player who does not anticipate will always find himself chasing the ball. (p. 68)

T f 50. One of the most important hints to playing a better game is: you should split your body in half; if the ball approaches on the left side take it with the left hand; if on the right side use the right arm. (p. 56)

T f 51. On your returns you should make a mental picture of the path that the ball will take. This will help make your shots more effective. (p. 56)

T f 52. When you are in doubt about your service you should serve to the corners and put spin on the ball. (p. 56)

T f 53. To play a more effective and efficient game and to be able to improve your playing ability it is necessary that you be able to analyze your skills and game. (p. 72)

T f 54. It is illegal to hit a served ball before it passes the short line even if it is still in the air. (p. 78)

t F 55. When a dead ball is called on the serve it is replayed without penalty and also eliminates any short or fault preceding this serve. (p. 78)

T f 56. An illegally served ball may not be played and must be re-served unless it is the second such short serve. (p. 78)

T f 57. A short is called if your partner is hit by the served ball on the bounce, unless he is standing outside the service box. (p. 78)

T f 58. In general, when trying to move out of the way of the ball you should move toward the center of the court. (p. 79)

t F 59. Hinders can occur between you and your partner as well as between you and your opponent. (p. 79)

t F 60. It is the duty of the side which is attempting to return the ball to stay out of the way of their opponents. (p. 79)

t F 61. There are several instances in which a court hinder entails a penalty. The penalty is a point or loss of service. (p. 80)

t F 62. It is not necessary to master the basic fundamentals of stroking and shot execution before you begin to develop strategic maneuvers. (p. 38)

T f   63. Most court play consists of a struggle to gain center court position which is considered the offensive position.   (p. 69)

T f   64. The server has the advantage in attaining center court position. Because of this the server should try for an ace or difficult to return service.   (p. 69)

T f   65. Handball when played on a high level of skill becomes a battle of the minds rather than a game requiring strength and speed.   (p. 72)

t F   66. If you are losing it is not a good idea to change your style of play but to concentrate more on execution of your shots.   (p. 71)

T f   67. To keep your opponent on the run and to force him to take difficult shots is one of the main objectives of four wall handball.   (p. 71)

t F   68. The best doubles teams are usually made up of the best singles players.   (p. 73)

t F   69. Talking to yourself during a game is a sign of poor game adjustment or a sign of inadequacy in playing ability.   (p. 72)

T f   70. Probably the most important objective in doubles is to assume front court position and to maintain it.   (p. 73)

T f   71. In doubles each member of a team should "play" each hit although only one will make the return hit.   (p. 73)

T f   72. During a rally in doubles the best position to assume is one in which each partner stands just back of the short line equidistant from each other and from the side wall.   (p. 74)

t F   73. Rallies in a game of doubles are usually shorter than in singles because of better court coverage.   (p. 74)

t F   74. The best arrangement for a team composed of a right- and a left-handed player is to have the left-handed player play the right side and the right-handed player to play the left side.   (p. 74)

t F   75. The side that has played the ball need not get out of the way of their opponents.   (p. 79)

COMPLETION

76. For the most effective hit you should step out at a (45) degree angle. (p. 12)

77. Another term for the fly hit is the (volley).   (p. 35)

78. An ace can only occur on a (the) (serve or service).   (p. 25)

79. The receiver must stand at least (five) feet behind the (short) line while the ball is being served.   (p. 78)

80. Another name for the diagonal serve is the (Z) serve.   (p. 23)

81. In the natural hop the ball breaks to the (left).   (p. 58)

82. Running long distances at a moderate rate is beneficial for development of (cardiorespiratory endurance).   (p. 51)

83. In stepping out to hit the ball you extend the ankle and knee joints and perform right hip abduction. This action is known as (stepping into the ball or getting your body into the hit).   (p. 12)

84. In order to rebound to the right the ball must have (counterclockwise) spin, when viewed from above.   (p. 14)

85. The roll out can only be witnessed in the (kill) shot.   (p. 28)

86. Stepping over the service line in the act of serving constitutes a (*fault*).
(p. 77)
87. In tournament play each player (or side) is allowed only (*three*) time outs.
(p. 78)
88. Your partner is hit by a served fly ball while standing in the service box. This counts as a (*dead ball*). (p. 78)
89. A ball which passes between your legs is called a (*straddled*) ball. (p. 79)
90. A (*screen ball*) occurs when the legally served ball returns from the front wall so close to the server that he obstructs your view of the ball. (p. 79)
91. The point is replayed whenever a (*hinder*) occurs. (p. 79)
92. A (*hinder*) occurs whenever you are unintentionally interfered with by your opponent in an attempt to return the ball. (p. 79)
93. A return of a ball that appeared to be impossible to return is termed a (*dig*).
(p. 80)
94. The game of "handball" in the Emerald Isle during the sixteenth and seventeenth centuries, came to be known as (*Fives*). (p. 1)
95. The organization, considered to be the players' fraternity, originated for and by the players is the (*United States Handball Association*) or as it is known in abbreviated form, the (*USHA*). (p. 3)
96. A three wall handball court which combines the one and four wall elements of play is known as the (*jai-alai*) type court. (p. 2)
97. The city known as the stronghold of the one-wall game for both men and women is (*New York*). (p. 3)
98. (*Western*) players put emphasis on court maneuvering and kills. (p. 3)
99. The (*one-wall*) game of handball is considered to be a truly American version.
(p. 2)
100. When the ball strikes the junction of the side wall and floor at the same time it is known as a (*crotch*) ball. (p. 25)
101. The two-wall kill is also known as the (*corner*) kill. (p. 28)

ANSWERS TO EVALUATION QUESTIONS

*No answer

Page	Answer and Page Reference

5. Four-wall, although at times, one-wall or three-wall play can be just as fast. This is due to the fact that the ball is in play more continuously because of the complete enclosure. Four wall provides for more varied play, followed by three wall and one wall. No back or side wall play in one wall. No back wall play in three wall.
14. Underspin (backspin), ball rebounds lower off the front wall. On right side, ball will have counterclockwise spin (viewed from above) and rebound to the right. You avoid spin by not using any wrist action. (pp. 13-14)
46. *Every day. Once-twice daily. Two-three times per week.
55. ***
82. Play the point over. The player who executes an illegal hit should call it.
(p. 81)

Index